"Virginia Herbers brings to life the nameless figures who prominently feature in Scripture and interact with Christ. Her effective and affecting invitation to encounter anew these important, if anonymous, people renders them and the lessons they offer in a provocative, contemporary, and meaningful way."

— Kerry Alys Robinson, Global Ambassador of the Leadership Roundtable

"While some may shrink from tackling the vexing questions and challenges of the human condition, Virginia Herbers courageously dives in with zeal. Relying on scholarship and imagination, she probes the complexities of biblical stories with refreshing honesty. The frank and candid manner in which she relates her own life experiences with those of the unnamed biblical characters makes this work pure delight to read."

— Annmarie Sanders, IHM, Communications Director, Leadership Conference of Women Religious

"Some writers convey deep spiritual and theological insights. Others are entrancing story tellers who can bring the Bible to life. It's rare to find both abilities in the very same author. Reading *Gifts from Friends We've Yet to Meet* is like swapping family stories with your cousin on a warm summer evening, both of you laughing and drinking good wine and learning things that will make you a better person."

— Paula Huston, author of *The Hermits of Big Sur*

"Through her skillful storytelling, Virginia invites us to weave the stories of nameless Gospel characters with our own story. Blending the tools of Scripture scholarship with insights gleaned from her own prayer and lived experience, she opens space for each of us to encounter a God eager to walk with us, eager to encourage us through the people placed along our path, friends known and those we've yet to meet."

— Kristin Matthes, SNDdeN, former chair of the National Religious Vocation Conference Board

"Virginia Herbers is a gifted teacher and storyteller—and just the right person to take us on a personal tour of some of the New Testament's lesser-known characters. From the Canaanite woman to the crucified thief, Herbers writes about these biblical figures as though she's met them—and indeed she has. Prepare to make some new friends—including Herbers herself—and receive the gifts they have to offer in this decidedly original, gently humorous, and deeply insightful book."

— Amy Ekeh, Director, Little Rock Scripture Study

"Through the tender and vulnerable stories of her own life, Herbers introduces us to the tender and vulnerable people of the Gospel, who in turn introduce us to the One who consecrates all our stories."

— Mark E. Thibodeaux, SJ, author of *Ascending with Ignatius*

"Virginia's writing style is so personable and draws you into her life and the lives of these biblical friends. Virginia encourages us to be bold yet humble when coming to the Father while challenging us to remain soft and compassionate for those hurting. If you are looking for a book to inspire and challenge you, this is it."

— Dedee Lhamon, founder of The Covering House

Gifts from Friends
We've Yet to Meet

A Memoir of Biblical Encounters

Virginia Herbers

LITURGICAL PRESS

Collegeville, Minnesota

www.litpress.org

2   3   4   5   6   7   8   9

Library of Congress Cataloging-in-Publication Data

Names: Herbers, Virginia, author.
Title: Gifts from friends we've yet to meet : a memoir of biblical encounters / Virginia Herbers.
Description: Collegeville, Minnesota : Liturgical Press, [2021] | Includes bibliographical references. | Summary: "Virginia Herbers introduces readers to nameless Gospel characters"—Provided by publisher.
Identifiers: LCCN 2021019242 (print) | LCCN 2021019243 (ebook) | ISBN 9780814666685 (paperback) | ISBN 9780814666692 (epub) | ISBN 9780814666692 (pdf)
Subjects: LCSH: Bible. Gospels--Biography.
Classification: LCC BS2430 .H47 2021 (print) | LCC BS2430 (ebook) | DDC 226/.0922—dc23
LC record available at https://lccn.loc.gov/2021019242
LC ebook record available at https://lccn.loc.gov/2021019243

To my beloved parents, Vincent and Janette Herbers,
who first taught me what God's love looks and acts like

Contents

Introduction

"What's your name again?" I always feel just a little stung when I realize I am unknown to someone I thought would remember me or upon whom I thought I had made a good impression. As the youngest child in a very large family, I grew up as one among many, part of the pack. I admittedly got more than my fair share of special attention being the youngest of thirteen kids (seven years younger than the sibling closest to me in age), but it was also a common occurrence to be called the wrong name by parent, teacher, pastor, or coach. Of course, there were occasions when this anonymity worked to personal advantage, as in the day when my mother, turning her back just long enough for me to get a forbidden mouthful of raw cookie dough, cried out with exasperation, "Rose, Joanie, Matthew, O child of grace, what is your name?" Usually, though, I desired recognition and personal affirmation much more than anonymity and interchangeability.

Having an experience of being unknown can hit a hollow spot in the soul, dropping like a stone and hitting with a soft but certain thud in the least secured landing of the heart. The feeling of being forgettable is one that requires a type of spiritual reckoning. In the gospels, the frequent occurrence of unnamed individuals is striking, even as their role in the life and ministry of Jesus is undeniably crucial. "The woman" at the well, "the friends" of the paralytic, "the centurion" whose faith heals his servant, "the demoniac" who recognizes Jesus as the Son of God: all are but a few of the dozens of gospel characters who figure prominently but anonymously in the life and mission of Jesus, even while others (such as Zacchaeus, Tabitha, Jairus) are named directly.

Scripture scholars have written much about the significance of those purposely named in the gospels as well as the social, political, and religious structures that would have prevented those same writers from naming others specifically.[1] Although these matters are intriguing to ponder, they are not the question of this book—our query is not academic or theological but personal. It is a question that affects *us now*, in relationship with *them then*. What is the role of the nameless figure (or collection of figures) in the life of Christ? What does it mean to be anonymous in the story of our God? Isn't God the one who calls us by name and knows us even before we are born? What does it mean to play a meaningful role in the story of our God and yet still be unidentified in that story? Isn't this a fear we each hold somewhere deep down, in a soul-place that is almost too vulnerable to access?

Have you ever worried that your life is not remarkable enough, important enough, or holy enough to get God's attention? Have you ever wondered if, when push comes to shove, you will be claimed by God? The worry might sound something like this: "Sure, God created me and gave me life, so of course God knew me in the beginning, when I was innocent and good. But at the end of my life, after everything I've done, will I be claimed by God? Does God remember me even now? Would God still choose me? Do I truly matter to God? When I pray, does God actually listen? Does God really know and care about what is happening in my singular little life? Maybe

---

[1] For a brief but delightful jaunt into this issue, I recommend Bruce M. Metzger, "Names for the Nameless," in *The Oxford Companion to the Bible*, ed. Bruce M. Metzger and Michael D. Coogan, *Oxford Biblical Studies Online*, http://www.oxfordbiblicalstudies.com/article/opr/t120/e0515 (accessed 08 Oct. 2020).

I won't make the cut in the end simply because I haven't done enough with what God has given me. Maybe I will have made such a mess of my life that God won't even recognize me."

(If your answer to these ponderings is "I've never really worried about things like that," then meeting the characters in this book may take you on a wild new adventure exploring faith and doubt, hope and fear.)

It seems that even the most devout of believers often harbors the same nagging questions: *What am I worth to God? Does God truly know me—the real me—and love me anyway?* We readily profess the head-answer to these questions: "Of course God knows me and loves me." But the soul's answer is not so simple, and even the saintliest of the saints have struggled with it.[2] Our very existence is evidence that God knows us and wants us; we can only exist because God has loved us into being. This we know and believe intellectually, but as our lives unfold, being known by God and being loved by God somehow cease to be felt as certainties for a lot of us. We begin to wonder whether our lives of faith are so unremarkable that we might find ourselves standing at the gate of heaven at the end of our lives only to hear him say, "What's your name again?"

Have you ever found yourself speaking with a customer service representative on the other end of the line who actually went out of her way to solve your problem with effectiveness and genuine kindness? Have you sat on a plane and discovered that the life of the person next to you intersected with yours in some inexplicable way? Have you heard a stranger make a random comment that was somehow a perfect insight into your life?

Encounters like these, with complete strangers, can change the direction of our attitudes, our behaviors, or even our very lives. When I was seventeen years old, I went to Australia over

---

[2] Perhaps the most well-known reference when we speak of these kinds of questions is St. John of the Cross and his "Dark Night of the Soul."

Christmas break to visit my sister, and I was plagued by the question of what to do with the rest of my life, convinced as many teenagers are that my lifelong happiness rested on the singular decision at that point in my life: where to go to college. I sat on a short stone wall in a decrepit church parking lot, all alone in a city and continent unknown to me, pondering the big life questions of meaning, choice, and vocation. Whether I wore the weight of the world on my face or not I can't say, but what I do know is that I was wishing that my granny, the wisdom figure of my life, was still alive because I would have laid out for her the entirety of my existential dilemma. She would have listened carefully before giving me her advice, and then I would have trusted her insight and judgment, knowing its source was nothing more or less than unselfish love. I sat on that Australian stone wall for about twenty minutes ruminating on possibility and longing, so caught up in the demands of my destiny that I didn't notice a middle-aged woman walking my way. I have no idea what her own world held that day, but when she walked past me, an unknown American girl sitting in her neighborhood, she looked at me, smiled, paused for just a moment as she walked past, and felt compelled to declare, "Darlin', you're going to be just fine. Trust your instincts." That was it. No greeting, no question, no introduction. Just that little statement with no explanation. I had been too stunned to even ask her name. An anonymous stranger, whose role in my life was fleeting but meaningful, offered to me that day the exact thing I needed. She couldn't have loved me—she didn't even know me—but her words struck to the core of my spirit, conveying the very compassion, wisdom, and love I needed in that moment. To this day, I call this life-changing character in my life my "Sydney granny." I wish I knew her name, but even without it, her place in my memory and in my life's journey remains undeniably meaningful.

So here are some more questions for us to ponder: What significance might an insignificant encounter have in the greater narrative of our lives? Who are the "anonymous figures" you've encountered who have played a critical role in your life? How do the experiences of the nameless gospel characters, whom we will never be able to specify in prayer or story, continue to reach and teach us today, not just in spite of their anonymity but actually *because* of it? Can it be that their anonymity allows for their experience to be not only personal but also universal? If we read a story from the gospels about Peter or Thomas or Judas, it is, of course, personal—between Jesus and that person. We can glean meaning and relevance from the story and the interaction, but somehow the experience remains historically fixed, allowing us to keep something of an easy distance from its impact. It doesn't necessarily feel universal in scope; it can easily feel specific to the person engaging with Jesus. But if I read a story about Jesus and "a boy" or "a woman," I have to contend with the question "What if that were me?" Gone is the luxury of letting myself off the hook because I'm not St. Peter, whose story and actions I can readily verify from source material, whose discipleship is trackable and thus not necessarily in sync with my own. Suddenly but subtly I myself have to *reckon* with every anonymous encounter on a personal level. I read it from a centuries-old Bible, and even though the interaction in the gospel story was certainly personal for the unnamed individual, it now also becomes personal for me. That which took place in Israel two thousand years ago crashes into every "here and now" since, making an ancient experience applicable to each person who reads it anew in his or her own circumstances. Anonymity thus becomes both personal *and* universal, and anonymous characters become our friends. Even without proper names, these folks share their stories with us and allow us to claim our place within those stories. They are dear friends we just haven't met yet, and each of their ages-old encounters with Jesus contains a gift for you and for me—today.

Did the gospel writers intentionally leave some of the characters in their narratives nameless so that we might insert ourselves in their place? That might be a stretch, but the fact of the matter is that these gospel friends we can't name had a role to play then, and I believe they have a role to play today, not just in the reading of Scripture but, maybe more importantly, in the application of it to our own experiences. Just like my Sydney granny, each of these people reminds us of who we are and who we can become in order to live more trustingly, more authentically, and more joyfully on this adventure called the Christian life. Let's get to know some of them a little bit better and see what gifts they might be offering us.

Chapter 1: Love Waits

A Gift from the Rich Young Man

Now someone approached him and said, "Teacher, what good must I do to gain eternal life?" He answered him, "Why do you ask me about the good? There is only One who is good. If you wish to enter into life, keep the commandments." He asked him, "Which ones?" And Jesus replied, " 'You shall not kill; you shall not commit adultery; you shall not steal; you shall not bear false witness; honor your father and your mother'; and 'you shall love your neighbor as yourself.' " The young man said to him, "All of these I have observed. What do I still lack?" Jesus said to him, "If you wish to be perfect, go, sell what you have and give to [the] poor, and you will have treasure in heaven. Then come, follow me." When the young man heard this statement, he went away sad, for he had many possessions.

— *Matthew 19:16-22*

ℬ

I've always felt kind of bad for this "rich young man."[1] He was so eager to be good, so ready to ask, "What else can I do?"

---

[1] Matthew doesn't specifically use the characterization "rich." We only read in v. 22 that he "had many possessions." He does, however, characterize him as "young." Interestingly, neither Mark nor Luke refer to him as young, but both characterize him as "rich." See Mark 10:17-22 and Luke 18:18-23.

I have known this feeling of enthusiasm, this desire to do more for God. And I have likewise known that in asking the question "How can I do even more for you, God?" the response I really hope to hear is a commendation, a pat on the back, something along the lines of "More? Heavens, you've done just fine as it is. Well done, my good and faithful servant! All that's left for you to do is wait for your eternal reward." Instead, Jesus answers the youngster in the story (and me, too, I imagine), "Oh? You don't just want the basic material; you actually want the honors class *and* the extra credit? Well, now you're talking!" Beyond that, he tells him that "the honors class" means giving up, giving over, and giving in, and then—*then*—coming back and saying yes to the role of lifelong discipleship. I can almost envision the young man's shoulders sagging, crestfallen that Jesus took him at his word and actually asked *more* of him than he was already doing. I have also known this feeling! My articulation of it runs along the following lines: "Dang. I was hoping I could have the prize without having to do anything *that hard* to get it."

It seems that this could have been the story of the calling of the thirteenth Apostle had the rich young man accepted Jesus' invitation. But his response was to walk away. The fact that the story ends here actually allows for the possibility that perhaps eventually he did become one of Jesus' disciples. My favorite theological speculation is that he is actually the "rich man from Arimathea named Joseph" who shows up eight chapters later in Matthew 27:57 to provide the newly hewn tomb for the body of the crucified Christ. That is, however, only speculation, and so in his namelessness (i.e., lack of historical verification), we are left to wrestle with the question of his choice—and thus also our own.

When I ponder the personal relevance of this encounter and take stock of my own "many possessions," I have to ask myself if they prevent me from saying yes to God's invitation to follow him more closely, more personally. I might not have possessions that amount to much in terms of wealth, but I shouldn't lull myself into the belief that I therefore am not "rich." What are the "many possessions" that I have, that *you* have? For me, I would say, first and foremost, books—so many books. The handwritten journals that I have kept over the years—over twenty volumes, actually. Music of all kinds. Digital files (ugh—let's not even talk about those). Pictures. Did I say books? These might not seem much like "possessions" to anyone else, but let me make two points.

First, these things have accumulated over time, and they represent my education, my leisure time, my hobbies, my work, my talents, my relationships—all things born out of and developed because of a certain degree of wealth and privilege, particularly when they are recognized as the outcome of opportunities that have been available to me that are unavailable to the vast majority of my brothers and sisters around the globe.[2] I, like the young man in this scene, am rich.

Second, it is important to distinguish riches from possessions. I know many a wealthy person who will give generously of their riches without a second thought; they are not possessive of their wealth and their wealth doesn't possess them. Likewise, there are things we have that, although not valuable from a monetary point of view, we cling to quite possessively. An example of my own is time. How generous am I with my time? How much do I weigh the request for it before I give it away? Do I deem some people more worthy of receiving it than others? Do I hoard it? Do I spend it only for my own purposes, or am I willing to "give it to the poor," as Jesus instructs? In reading this gospel passage, I know immediately that one of my "many possessions" is my time—it possesses me more than I possess it. If Jesus looked at me and my schedules and

[2] A few statistical examples worth pondering include the finding that less than 7 percent of the world's population has a college degree and more than 60 percent lack internet access. For more information, see https://www.100people.org/index.php.

calendars and asked me to surrender all of it in order to follow him more closely, I wonder how eager I would be to do so. Would I also go away sad, ruminating on how unreasonable his request was? Would I think, "What would happen to all the commitments I've made, the people who are counting on me, my responsibilities"?

Point of fact: God *does* ask me to do this—often! Once when I was sitting down to meet a swiftly approaching deadline for a column, my phone rang and I picked up the call from a friend, thinking it would be a quick two-minute hello, ending with my promise to call back when I had more time to chat. Instead, I was met with sobs on the other end of the line. When she was finally able to tell the story, it was one of tragedy, the sudden loss of her sister on the anniversary of her father's death. "Can you come?" she asked. I am embarrassed to admit that, for as good a friend as she was to me, I hesitated. Despite the fact that I did go immediately after hanging up, that first hesitation was not negligible. There was the "cry of the poor" on the other end of the line—unmistakable, needy, urgent—and there I was, weighing it against my own personal time and agenda.

As I compose this chapter, I do so from the isolation that COVID-19 has brought to our world. Talk about having our life's plans and timelines interrupted! The entire human race is struggling with the effects of being *forced* to change our plans, our expectations, our priorities. We are being force-fed a lesson in letting go of the control we thought we had. I, for one, have not received it with the saintly acceptance and gratitude that I wish I had, but I certainly do recognize the invitation being offered from God: *Let go. Control has always been one of your preferred illusions anyway. Give your plans to me. Let me have them.*

Life with Christ rarely syncs well with calendars and schedules. "Kairos," or God's time, is distinct from "chronos," chronological time. Kairos is the time it takes for a piece of fruit to become ripe or the sense you might have at family dinner that the right time to raise a difficult issue has come. It cannot be scheduled, predicted, or controlled like chronos can. God's kairos is what shows up most frequently in the Scriptures—everywhere from his appearance to Elijah as the "tiny whispering sound" (see 1 Kgs 19:12) to Jesus' launching his public ministry in Cana where, incidentally, his mother Mary sensed that it was his time to "get going" before Jesus did (see John 2:1-12).

God doesn't work on our schedules, grace doesn't come on command, and the cry of the poor isn't heard according to a predetermined itinerary. Personally, I might prefer adding in "mystical experiences" and "spiritual works of mercy" to my regularly scheduled programming so that I can ensure that they will be convenient, sanitary, and socially acceptable. But the fact of the matter is that I am in for a surprise when I come to prayer at the end of the day saying, "Hello, Lord. Today I have honored my father and mother, refrained from bearing false witness, and not stolen anything. What more can I do for you tomorrow?" God might just answer me the same way Jesus replied to the rich young man: "Well, how about you take the rest of the month's agenda and toss it; then, open your eyes and ears to the spontaneous needs that I keep putting right in front of you?" I guarantee my response would not be an automatic "OK, great! Thank you so much, my great God, for choosing me, your humble servant, for these opportunities!" It would be, I confess, more steeped with protests about long-standing appointments or important meetings or maybe with mild panic about how to manage the uncertainty of such a life. I might even become defensive about the impracticality and disrespect of not abiding by other people's needs and schedules! First, I'd likely go away sad, and then I might stomp around, a little bit mad. I am the rich young man, and he is me.

The story of either the rich young man or me, whichever you'd prefer to entertain, needn't end there, though, despite the fact that the Scripture passage does. He goes away sad, but does he ever come back again? Do I? Would you? The namelessness of this rich young man becomes an invitation to us, and we are asked to replace his anonymity with our reality and give an answer. Today. Now. Maybe it's not pretty. Maybe it's the same answer he gave: drooping our heads and walking away sad, mumbling excuses for why it inevitably has to be this way. Just like his story, though, ours needn't end with that initial response.

I believe there is a hidden lesson about God in the life snippet of this rich young man, and it is this: Love waits. We are left in the gospel with the man's sad departure, but Jesus' invitation stands, and it is up to both our imagination and our own life choices to determine whether or not a return ever occurs. Maybe I go away sad and then become mad for a little while, but then what? *Then what?* One thing I believe pretty certainly is that the rich young man couldn't unhear Jesus' invitation, couldn't unknow the call to discipleship. Sure, he could work to forget it, try to dull the memory or numb the pain of having refused the invitation, but encountering Jesus is not one moment among many in a person's lifetime. Encountering Jesus is definitional. I can't help but believe that the echo of Christ's invitation resounded in the heart and mind of this young man until he simply couldn't ignore it any longer. Perhaps there was a second definitional moment—the moment of decision and ultimate response *after* he went away sad. Did he stop resisting the steep price tag and ultimately decide to "give it all away," or did he instead determine once and for all to silence the invitation's echo, settling for living a "good enough" life?

It would not be unreasonable to imagine that he might have chosen to focus on just the first part of the conversation, remembering Jesus' affirmation with regard to all the commandments he had kept throughout his youth. After all, Jesus was clear in the first part of his response. What the rich young man had done "from his youth" (Mark 10:20) was exactly what God requires, Jesus said. That feels like a pat on the back; that feels like affirmation. "Good for you!" Jesus seemed to say.

But in the actual event, the conversation didn't stop there. So did he choose to remember only that he had asked a simple question and gotten a simple answer at first, considering that "good enough"? Or did his memory of the second part of the conversation haunt him, forcing him to battle his internal rationalizations? Might he have finally given in to that tormenting memory, ending his resistance to Jesus' invitation to sell all? Isn't it possible that one day later he did indeed decide to surrender, responding to Jesus' call to "come, follow me" in discipleship?

What our imaginative prayer tells us about the rich young man reveals what we need to know about *ourselves*. The rich young man went away that day, but Jesus stayed, loving him still and always. And I believe he waited. Love waits for us to opt in.

At my childhood home, our backyard consisted of a concrete patio, a garage, and a grass patch only big enough to grow a few tomato plants. To maintain some degree of sanity in the hot summer months for both adults and children, my parents purchased a family membership to a local swimming pool. Dad would often pile at least some of his thirteen children into the station wagon after dinner to spend a few precious hours enjoying summer evenings at the pool, giving my poor ragged mother a break. One of these nights stands out very clearly in my memory.

I was almost five years old, and I wanted to experience the same kind of reckless abandon that I observed in my older siblings as they ran headlong to the edge of the pool and hurled their bodies (or some other sibling's) into the water. I hadn't learned how to swim well yet, so I wasn't allowed in the deep end, but I wanted to at least jump into the shallows like my demigod siblings instead of cautiously walking down the steps holding my dad's hand.

I must have expressed this desire aloud because my sister Clare, eight years my senior, took it upon herself to help me.

She stood in the three-foot-deep end of the pool with outstretched arms and promised, "Go ahead and jump. I'm right here." Excited and eager but frightened as well, I paced back and forth along the edge of the pool, considering the prospect. There she was, my trustworthy older sister, ensuring that I would be OK, encouraging me to trust, waiting for me to be ready. And there I was, pacing and deliberating and stalling. I remember taking a long time to make the move, and I also remember Clare's long vigil from inside the shallow end, arms open to catch me. She was the embodiment of "love waiting."

"You're going to pull me up if I go under?" I asked.

"Yes."

Think, approach, squat, worry.

"What if I can't touch bottom?"

"You've been in this end of the pool before. You'll be OK."

Nod, approach, crouch, stall.

"Is it really cold?"

"Nope."

Stand, inspect the scab on my knee, observe the ants on the sidewalk.

"Virginia, are you going to jump or not?"

"Maybe I should just use the steps."

"Whatever you want," she said as she dropped her arms. (As I recall this memory now, I am in awe of how patient my twelve-year-old sister was with me. She remains, to this day, one of the most patient human beings I believe God has ever created.)

"OK, I want to jump," I resolved.

"OK." Arms back up.

Crouch, tense, prepare, delay.

"It'll be OK? You're going to stay there and catch me?" I fretted.

More firmly now: "Yes, already!"

And then, at the thought that the opportunity might disappear, I stopped catastrophizing and jumped, landing anticlimactically with an understated *sploosh*.

Love waits. Through our fear and worry and even delay, it waits. If a twelve-year-old big sister can keep vigil at the side of a swimming pool with tired arms, just imagine what God can do, even when we "[walk] away sad." When we fear and worry about the choices before us, what does God do? It seems, both in the story of the rich young man and in our own stories now, that God waits. He respects our ability to say no—and our potential to eventually say yes. He waits, knowing that for as real as the "no" might be, the I've-changed-my-mind-I'm-coming-wait-for-me "yes" is all the sweeter.

Did the rich young man come back to Jesus at some later date? I'm one of those who believes he did.

I have absolutely no memory of anything at the swimming pool after my famous summer jump except that I did indeed survive and don't think I ever used the stairs again. My guess is that in finding the experience—and my sister—trustworthy, all the fear leaked out of it and I moved on to bigger and better things—jumping into the deep end, off the diving board, and then, eventually, off the back of a boat into open waters. Fear is a deceptive thing. It looms so large, rattles such noisy chains, wields power too big for words. What was I fearing from the edge of that pool? Death or injury? I don't remember, but I doubt it was that dramatic. If I was anything then like I am now, I was probably fearing the unknown and the untried.

What was the rich young man fearing or resisting in the face of Jesus' invitation? Maybe the same thing: the unknown and the untried. "What will happen?" "Will I be OK?" "What will this cost me, and can I really give it all up?" Those aren't questions just from him; they're our questions, too. "Can I do this?" "Is it worth it?" "What if . . .?"

Love waits for us to decide, allowing the last syllable of our protest to fade away, keeping vigil until we take one last deep breath and choose, finally, to jump.

Chapter 2: Beyond Rejection

A Gift from the Canaanite Woman

Then Jesus went from that place and withdrew to the
region of Tyre and Sidon. And behold, a Canaanite woman
of that district came and called out, "Have pity on me,
Lord, Son of David! My daughter is tormented by a
demon." But he did not say a word in answer to her.
His disciples came and asked him, "Send her away, for
she keeps calling out after us." He said in reply, "I was
sent only to the lost sheep of the house of Israel." But the
woman came and did him homage, saying, "Lord, help
me." He said in reply, "It is not right to take the food of the
children and throw it to the dogs." She said, "Please, Lord,
for even the dogs eat the scraps that fall from the table of
their masters." Then Jesus said to her in reply, "O woman,
great is your faith! Let it be done for you as you wish."
And her daughter was healed from that hour.

— *Matthew 15:21-28*

❀

This is a tough one. I have known only a very few preach-
ers who have dared to take this particular Scripture story head-
on, and I'm sorry to say that it has rarely come off well. The
few sermons I have heard usually do one of two things. Either
they attempt to justify Jesus' calling this unnamed woman a

dog by appealing to the societal norms of the day, or they try to soften the blow and theorize that Jesus had intended to heal her all along and was just using a dramatic exchange to get the attention of the disciples. Unconvincing, both.

One of my early theology teachers taught me that when I find a Scripture passage particularly galling (as I find this one), I would do well to wrestle with it until it blesses me. Study it, pray with it, talk about it, research it, argue with it, rant about it, but don't abandon it. Well, I struggled with this passage for the better part of two decades before its blessing emerged, but when it came, it came fast and sure. The blessing from this anonymous Canaanite woman is undeniable in my own spiritual life, and I venture to say her blessing can reach into the life of anyone who has ever felt ignored, rejected, or scorned by God—because hers is a blessing that arises from the spiritual wasteland of those very emotions.

This woman remembered the goodness of God when even God seemed to have forgotten how to be good. Her persistence and her memory formed the faith that reversed Jesus' rejection. Look carefully at his response to her pleas. First, he ignored her; then, his reply likened her to an animal. We must wrestle with both Jesus' silence and his apparently demeaning words toward this woman if we are ever to obtain the blessing within the experience, both hers and ours. It doesn't help to sugarcoat or rationalize Jesus' behavior. His words and action come across as, quite frankly, rude. Ungodly, if you will.

How do we explain Jesus' seemingly cold and dehumanizing response to this person in need? It is antithetical not only to what we know about the person of Jesus but also to what he had been saying and doing immediately prior to this exchange! Earlier in this same chapter, Jesus had been critical of the religious leaders, calling them hypocrites for their strict interpretation of law over and above the needs of the people before them. Immediately preceding this passage, Jesus had taught his disciples about the dangers of legalism, with no slight amount of exasperation: "Hear and understand. It is not what enters one's mouth that defiles that person; but what comes out of the mouth is what defiles one. . . . But the things that come out of the mouth come from the heart, and they defile" (Matt 15:10-11, 18). Then, in the very next encounter, a mere eight verses later, the words that "come out of [his] mouth" are words that characterize this woman as a dog. Do these words "come from the heart" of Jesus, expressing the belief that this woman deserves to be treated in such a way? Is he claiming exclusion from the self-defilement of these words based on the fact that the woman is not Jewish? Did he forget what he had just said, or was he not considering the attribution "dog" as negative? Was he drawing a line of demarcation for where God's love and mercy stop and start? No, no, no, and no.

All throughout Matthew's gospel, Jesus heals the blind and lame, the demon-possessed, foreigners, sinners, women, children, religious and irreligious alike. So why did this particular exchange with this particular woman evoke this particular response? Considering the context just explained, it couldn't have been about her gender nor about the legal tenets of her social or religious standing. So . . . *what in the world?*

Most scholars agree that Matthew's gospel was written for early converts to Christianity, mostly Jews. Matthew's portrayal of Jesus consistently confirms for his readers that Jesus is the one who fulfills the prophecies of the Old Testament, that he is the Messiah long-awaited by the Jewish people. Matthew's gospel has multiple references that would have been immediately recognizable as rooted in the Old Testament— everything from the opening chapter situating Jesus' descendancy in the "family tree" of Abraham and King David to Jesus' utterance of Psalm 22 in Hebrew when he was dying on the cross. Throughout the entirety of his gospel, Matthew draws parallels between the Old Testament action of God in the life of Israel and the ministry and choices of the Christ, indicating the nature of the "new covenant" for the "new Israel" in the "new promised land" of God's "new kingdom." The encounter in chapter 15 is no exception. What God had done for Israel, the "chosen people" in the Old Testament, serves as the backdrop for Matthew's understanding of what Jesus is doing here. So who is the "new Israel"? Who is Jesus indicating the "chosen people" will be at the inbreaking of God's eternal kingdom?

Enter the Canaanite woman.

Let's set the stage for this exchange.

The location is Tyre and Sidon, one of the most dangerous regions in the Old Testament histories.[1] Inference: Jesus is in dangerous territory, both literally and figuratively.

The main character is a Canaanite, Israel's sworn enemy from the earliest moments of salvation history. Inference: there is no worthiness to this request; it comes from an enemy—and a woman, no less! This person need not be acknowledged, much less appeased.

The situation is the demonic possession of a young girl, someone with no social or religious status and with no apparent advocate besides her mother. Inference: this person has no value; godless people don't get to make claims on God.

When Jesus ignores the entreaty of the woman for her daughter and then, after her persistence, goes on to imply that she is not within the scope of his ministry, we are left bewildered by his behavior and words, at a loss with regard to the inferences made from them. Despite the fact that an observant Jew of his day might have legitimately acted this way, Jesus' behavior does not reflect the Jesus we expect after reading the first fourteen chapters of Matthew. This is a Jesus who requires either our excusal or our reckoning.

Gail R. O'Day, a New Testament professor and ordained minister of the United Church of Christ, wrote an article several

---

[1] Tyre and Sidon were ancient cities considered to be enemies of Israel and objects of God's displeasure (see Isaiah 23 and Ezekiel 26–28 for starters).

years ago that was essential in helping me through my own personal wrestling match with the Jesus in this passage.[2] In her article, O'Day draws a comparison between Matthew's depiction of Jesus' exchange with this Canaanite woman and the Old Testament lament psalms. Her arguments are complex, and we cannot venture too far into the intricacies of her exposition of Scriptural theology here; nevertheless, several of her insights are helpful. She points out that the Old Testament laments follow a particular form that is discernible in the words of the Canaanite woman and would likely have been apparent to the original receivers of Matthew's gospel.[3] I cannot do justice here to the form criticism of either this passage or lament psalms as a whole,[4] but in what follows I offer some general elements of a lament worth considering briefly:

1. The speaker of a lament is in a wretched state, often because of his own doing (sin, infidelity, etc.) and speaks his plea to God in desperate tones.

2. In addressing God, the speaker of a lament persists through God's lack of response, acknowledging that God's refusal to act may well be justified in light of the petitioner's infidelity.

3. The lamenter provides rationale to God as to why his plea ought to be heard and why God ought to act with mercy.

4. The plea gives way to words of trust in God's faithfulness (thus assuming God will respond positively to the lamenter's request) and of praise for God's unconditional love.

---

[2] Gail R. O'Day, "Surprised by Faith: Jesus and the Canaanite Woman," *Listening/Journal of Religion and Culture* 24 (1989): 290–301.

[3] Psalm 13 offers a clear and succinct example of this form.

[4] For two excellent sources, see Claus Westermann's *Praise and Lament in the Psalms* (Atlanta: John Knox Press, 1981), and Walter Brueggemann's *The Message of the Psalms* (Minneapolis: Augsburg Fortress, 1984).

O'Day believes it is precisely the lament psalm that Matthew is mirroring in the exchange between Jesus and the Canaanite woman. With this in mind, we have a way to engage with this anonymous character personally. If this passage is reminiscent of the Old Testament laments, then it is connected to the entire story of our life in God. And if it is connected to the entire story of our life in God, then *we* are connected to it in ways that take us beyond the role of mere spectator. Our Canaanite sister becomes the actor in a scene that is situated in the entirety of salvation history, drawing that history into her own circumstances and making a claim on it as an insider. If she is, as O'Day theorizes, echoing a lament in the tradition of ancient Jewish heritage, then she *belongs,* and the lament is the very vehicle serving to prove it—even to Jesus. In uttering a lament to God, this nameless woman claims her place as "one of us," and in so doing, her plea becomes the chamber into which our own laments echo, even today. For any of us who feel outside God's reach, beyond the limits of God's mercy, it is as if she's reminding us of our place: *No, dear. You belong. You are God's and God is yours. Make your claim.*

Who is this woman, this "Canaanite woman" of our ancestry?

To the disciples—and ostensibly even to Jesus—she is a pariah. She approaches from a territory that evokes a sense of danger and threat, already putting everyone in the scene on edge. Then, she has the nerve to make a request of Jesus. She is a foreigner, an enemy. She has no claim to anything Jewish, much less to the powers of physical healing from him whom she herself calls "Son of David."

Step one of her lament: in desperation, she makes her need known to God.

"But he did not say a word in answer to her" (v. 23).

Step two of her lament: When ignored, she does not remain silent. Instead, *she persists*: "Lord, help me" (v. 25). She calls God by name and states her case.

"He said in reply, 'It is not right to take the food of the children and throw it to the dogs'" (v. 26).

Step three of her lament: she remains engaged despite God's seeming rejection. She reminds God of God's own promises and holds steady to her end of the relationship. She provides the explanation for why it's a good idea for God to grant the request.

Permit me to digress for a moment. An entertaining example of this element of lament comes from a notebook I kept during a Psalms class with Walter Brueggemann at the University of Notre Dame in June 2007. My handwritten notes from his lecture on Psalm 74 say this:

"The psalmist cannot help himself; he is dependent upon God's restoration and redemption. And yet he has been, admittedly, unfaithful. How is he to approach God in this conundrum? Ahhh . . . remind God of who God is in the first place and give a reason for him to act! 'Hey, you are God, and we are your chosen people. We didn't ask to be chosen. *You* chose *us*. Therefore, even if we sin, even if we are unfaithful, we are yours. You chose us. We might break the covenant but you can't. You're God and we are not. You chose us. And it wouldn't look good to your enemies if they thought you were a God who chooses poorly or who is unfaithful. Wouldn't that spell victory for the unbelievers, victory for your foes? But if you save us—that would demonstrate your power and glory, your magnificence and benevolence. They would see that you are God, only and true. So we praise you now, in anticipation of your coming glory, O God, all powerful. We await your arrival and will praise you until then. Sincerely, Israel.'"

Even more to the point, when Brueggemann was lecturing on the lament of Psalm 22, specifically the psalmist's cry in verse 7, "But I am a worm, not [human], / scorned by [everyone], despised by the people," my scribbled lecture notes say this: "Can't you just hear the psalmist saying, 'Yes, Lord, I am a worm, but I am *your worm*! You chose us to be your people so we are your responsibility—you must listen!' The response of God to this plea of lament comes in Isaiah 41:14: 'Fear not, O worm Jacob, O maggot Israel; I will help you!' 'Yes,' the Lord God is saying, 'do not be afraid! You are a worm, but you are *my worm!*' "

Brueggemann's explanation of this third element of the lament psalm is colorful, earthy, and absolutely *significant*—when God has reason to reject us for our infidelities and sin, we must remember that we are God's chosen, and it would serve us well to remind God of that reality! God is the one who chose us, so essentially, we are his responsibility whether he likes it or not. If he rejects us, doesn't that imply that he made a mistake in choosing us in the first place? Wouldn't acting with forgiveness and mercy be more authentic to the kind of loving god God claims to be? *This* is how God's chosen ones provide the rationale for why it is in God's best interests to actually act as God. We must claim our place as God's chosen and call on God to claim his place as *chooser*. And we must do so not only with deep faith but with deep humility; this is not an act of entitlement—this is an act of mutual fidelity.

Now, let's return to the Canaanite woman. She is quite cunning in this aspect of providing a reason for Jesus to act on her behalf. She uses Jesus' own words to provide the rationale. "Call me a dog? Well, OK, but I'm the dog at *your table*. And feeding *your* dog is *your* responsibility." Can't you just picture Jesus grinning at the cleverness—and even the audacity—of this verbal volley, particularly if he is recognizing the situation as reflective of Israel's laments? And can't you likewise picture the jaw-dropping that was happening among the disciples? This "enemy of Israel" was making a claim on the healing power that Jesus had reserved for "the house of Israel" and was doing so in the voice of the ancient prophets!

Step four of a lament is typically when the plea gives way to praise for God's faithfulness and action on the psalmist's behalf. However, O'Day notices that, if this gospel text follows the form of a lament, then something startling has occurred: the praise at the end of this exchange does not come from the woman toward God. The praise comes from the mouth of Jesus, the Son of God, *in honor of the woman's faith*. Simultaneous with these words of praise from Jesus is the healing of the Canaanite woman's daughter. This healing then opens the door for even fuller praise of God—from Canaanites, disciples, onlookers, all.

The community's praise of God is preceded by Jesus' praise for this woman's belief that she was already included in the covenant. "The Canaanite woman knows who Jesus is and holds him to it; she will not settle for a diminishment of the promise. She insists that Jesus be Jesus, and through her insistence she frees him to be fully who he is."[5]

Maybe this sounds too highfalutin for most of us non-theologians in the real world. What do form criticism and Old Testament lament psalms really have to do with the here and now? Well, the experience of feeling ignored, denied, or scorned by God is, unfortunately, relegated neither to first-century experience nor to theological academia. It is all too familiar in precisely the here and now. But what if that experience of God's absence is actually the very confirmation of our life in God's ongoing presence and our claim on membership in God's kingdom?

What are we to make of God's silence in the face of our desperate prayers? How are we to respond when we hear, resounding in that silence, the accusation of our own unworthiness or infidelities? In the midst of these experiences, pious platitudes are unsatisfactory at best and harmful at worst. God's silence is not a figment of our imagination, but neither is it a punishment for our failings. Sometimes we cannot perceive anything but God's absence. Desperate pleas, as the Canaanite woman understands, can be met with silence. Persistent

---

[5] O'Day, "Surprised by Faith," 301.

prayer, as she knows all too well, can be met with rejection. "No," God sometimes says. And even worse than "No," sometimes God's only response is deafening silence.

And yet . . .

Our Canaanite sister is our companion through these experiences. She witnesses to the pain of rejection, the desperation of our very souls, and the fear of all things uncertain. She stays with us as we cry to God, "Please hear me . . . please answer me . . . please," and she holds us as we wait for God's response. She is all too familiar with the vulnerability of that waiting. She keeps vigil with us in the void as witness to the fact that *everyone belongs*. She encourages us in the wake of God's silence to try again, to speak our truth, remembering who God is, relying on what God has promised, keeping our hearts open despite the risk, staying faithful. On our behalf, she does battle with the voices that accuse us of being unworthy and unwanted. She whispers to us, with a hint of chutzpah, "One more time, dearie." And she gets us back on our feet to remind God of who God is. She charges us to claim our place in the life of God once and for all. Our prayer becomes bolder then. More audacious. *We are yours, God. Like it or not, we are yours and it's your job to take care of us. Do your job.*

Speaking to God in prayer like this is anything but insolent; it is an act of utter and courageous faith. We believe God will act, or at the very least we believe we will have a hearing. We might not see results immediately, but we know God has received us. Staying in the conversation rights our relationship with God, and it rights God's relationship with us. It allows us to stand up, brush ourselves off, and go about our own business, letting God go about God's.

When I was in my early twenties, I was trying to decide whether or not I wanted to profess vows as a religious sister. I had entered the convent and moved to Connecticut immediately after graduating from high school (thanks again, Sydney Granny!) and was now looking at the prospect of taking religious vows. I wanted God to provide some kind of divine revelation about what the totality of my life was supposed to hold. A billboard, a chariot in the sky, anything would do. I didn't think such a request was unreasonable at the time, but I have since come to believe that God must be amused by these. Or maybe just amused by me.

On a walk one day, I was talking out loud to God about this desire for a sign, and we came to an agreement. We cut a deal, so to speak. It went like this: since our partnership consisted of one human (me) and one God (God), when the human party was at a weak point of faith in the God party, the God party would send on a flight of fancy a cardinal bird as an assurance to the human party that everything was going to be OK and that, yes, the God party was indeed paying attention and taking care of the human party. Seeing this lovely red harbinger, the human party would then trust the God party implicitly. At least in theory. For a little while.

This deal worked out pretty well, actually, especially during the years I was stationed in geographies where cardinals are plentiful. Whether their appearances were the stuff of God or the stuff of ornithology didn't really matter much to me—they served to bolster my faith and renew my trust. Like I said, at least for a little while.

After several years had passed without ever really putting this agreement to the test, I was transferred back to St. Louis to teach high school theology. I was thrilled to be back in my hometown. Soon, though, things started to go sideways. My mom had the first of several heart failures, one of my dearest friends contracted cancer, terrorist attacks besieged our nation, and clergy abuse scandals erupted not only all throughout the US church but also very close to home. In the course of just a few weeks, it felt to me as if the world had gone off its axis and there was no way to get a footing.

One day, in the midst of all this, I was desperate to attain some level of normalcy, so I went for a ride to pick up a birthday card for a friend. I took advantage of the privacy of the car ride to have another out-loud conversation with God about the current state of things. I did most of the talking—and by "most of," I mean all. I ranted and I raged, giving God a piece of my mind and proceeding to let God know that I thought he was doing a very lousy job of being God. I gave him some ridiculous ultimatum and reminded him of his end of the "God party" deal, saying (and I remember this as if it were this morning), "And if you were *ever* going to send a cardinal, you'd better make it right now and you'd better make it a big fat one!" Then, I waited for that bird to fly right into the car and perch on the dashboard.

Not only did God fail to send a cardinal in response to my demand, but he went one better and didn't even bother to help me remember where I was. The turn I needed to make to get to the store was upon me, and not only was I in the wrong lane, but there was no hope of getting into the left turn lane because the light I was approaching was turning yellow and I was in the far-right lane.

"Thanks a lot, God. You're a real pal. You really should work a little harder at being the all-caring, all-loving God you purport to be."

I was pretty worked up as I approached the intersection, looking over my left shoulder to see if I could cut across two lanes to make the turn. When it was clear that I couldn't, I huffed in exasperation and faced forward again. I was singularly focused on trying to think of a different route to the store just as I was coming to a stop at the light that was now red. When the car came to a halt at the intersection, Fredbird (the mascot of the St. Louis Cardinals baseball team) jumped into the crosswalk right in front of my car as part of a promotion the team was having at the corner gas station. Fredbird himself was giving out Cardinals paraphernalia and proceeded to motion for me to open the window so that he could toss in a Cardinals' hacky sack.

Fredbird. The biggest, fattest cardinal a girl could ask for. And a hacky sack. Just because.

Did I realize that day that I was participating in an ancient Jewish lament? Nope. I was just engaging God in the very real circumstances of my life and stating my case in the earthiest way possible. Earthy = real. And real = trusting.

Making demands on God's promises isn't necessarily impertinent. It can be an act of faith. We can't cry out to God unless we actually have hope that God might hear us. Our prayers, our demands, our insistences are a desperate plea for God to listen—*but they are born out of the belief that God is already listening*. Herein lies the distinction between these types of laments and acts of entitlement. Lament believes; entitlement demands.

Looking at it now, I was the Canaanite woman that day in the car, in every possible way. Now don't get me wrong. My friend's cancer didn't go away, the clergy sex abuse scandal didn't disappear, and life didn't suddenly become a bed of roses. But it seemed to me that God "remembered" how to be God in our relationship and I remembered how to be the "human party"—i.e., not God. My desperate plea did not ultimately go unheard or unheeded, despite my initial perception. What I perceived as God's "gotcha" in "not even helping me get in the right lane, for crying out loud" was, in fact, a critical element of how God would reveal himself to me in ways undeniable and unpredictable, assuring me that, yes, I am God's and God is mine. "It won't be the lane you asked for, but it will be the lane that will avail you of my love, over and above what you can possibly imagine. Just wait till you see what I have in store for you today," said God.

Not only was God listening, but he was playing a little, too. And I could have sworn that as the hacky sack hit the empty seat next to me, I heard, ever so faintly, the slight chuckle of my Canaanite sister, too. God, the Canaanite woman, and Fredbird: my very own trinitarian conspiracy, ratifying my place in the life of God, situating me in a long ancestral faith line and reminding me that *I belong*.

My prayer that night was quieter, gentler, softer. I might have even called it praise.

Chapter 3: Never Enough

A Gift from the Boy with the Five Loaves and Two Fish

Jesus went across the Sea of Galilee [of Tiberias]. A large crowd followed him, because they saw the signs he was performing on the sick. Jesus went up on the mountain, and there he sat down with his disciples. The Jewish feast of Passover was near. When Jesus raised his eyes and saw that a large crowd was coming to him, he said to Philip, "Where can we buy enough food for them to eat?" He said this to test him, because he himself knew what he was going to do. Philip answered him, "Two hundred days' wages worth of food would not be enough for each of them to have a little [bit]." One of his disciples, Andrew, the brother of Simon Peter, said to him, "There is a boy here who has five barley loaves and two fish; but what good are these for so many?" Jesus said, "Have the people recline." Now there was a great deal of grass in that place. So the men reclined, about five thousand in number. Then Jesus took the loaves, gave thanks, and distributed them to those who were reclining, and also as much of the fish as they wanted. When they had had their fill, he said to his disciples, "Gather the fragments left over, so that nothing will be wasted." So they collected them, and filled twelve wicker baskets with fragments from the five barley loaves that had been more than they could eat.

— John 6:1-13

ᎶᎦ

There is greatness in smallness. We see this theme over and over in the Scriptures: the scrawny youth David defeats the giant Goliath; God elects the "lost remnant of Israel"[1] to be the chosen people; the Messiah comes from Bethlehem, the smallest of Judah's clans; the single lost sheep becomes the chief object of concern to the shepherd of the flock. Added to these examples is this story about the feeding of the multitudes. The hero in this event is not one of the famous twelve apostles but an uncredentialed boy. Imagine this youngster, just one of the crowd who had come to see this healer named Jesus of Nazareth and maybe hear him preach. Who knows if he had already heard of this man or had a family member who had been healed by him? What we do know is that this young man showed up on that hillside with lunch packed, apparently prepared to make a day of it. And we know that he did not give much credence to the notion of scarcity. He lived out of a sense of bounty, a theology of abundance.

The initial details of the scene are pretty vivid: thousands of people had gathered on the side of a mountain near the Sea of Galilee, the disciples had gauged their numbers and assessed their need, and (at least according to John) a somewhat coy Jesus proceeded to ask a provocative question of Philip about where to buy them some food. Philip had his eyes firmly fixed on mathematics, logic, practicalities: a theology of efficiency. Philip and I would have been friends. The evangelist made Philip's response to Jesus tidier and more respectful than I imagine it might have been. Isn't it plausible to imagine that today's translation of his response to Jesus' question might be more along the lines of "Enough food for them? We wouldn't

[1] The "faithful remnant," or the *anawim*, references the people of Israel who were called by God to become the chosen people in the Hebrew Scriptures (see Zeph 3:12).

have enough even if we cleared out every deli in the neighborhood!" Jesus was not being reasonable, plain and simple.

Philip's statement that "Two hundred days' wages worth of food would not be enough for each of them to have a little [bit]" was true. The problem was just that it focused on something other than what held Jesus' attention. Philip was looking at the lack, on the provisions they *didn't* have. What the disciples had was insufficient, no two ways about it. *Lord, we don't have enough; it's not enough. Look at all these people. We can't do it.* Yes, Philip and I would have definitely been friends (I am practically certified in the theology of economy). Efficiency and practicality, however, were not the order of the day on this hillside in Galilee.

First batter out; next batter up.

Andrew came forward with a slightly better approach, bringing with him the little "loaves and fishes" guy. He at least acknowledged that there was potentiality in the single-portion lunch brought by the youngster, but then (maybe because he's Peter's brother, as the gospel writer ironically points out), he botched it with the doubtful addition: "but what good are these for so many?" Andrew would be a friend of mine, too, with this theology of uncertainty. Just when he might have had the perfect response of faith in Jesus, he balked and fell back on pragmatism. Can't you picture Jesus closing his eyes, dropping his head, and letting out a long, weary exhale? *So close; you were so close.*

Second batter out.

But then comes the boy, and he was, I believe, the one really worth befriending. Where did he come from anyway? Had he been standing there the whole time? Did he overhear Jesus' question to Philip? Had he watched and heard enough from Jesus to sense that something incredible was about to happen? Did he know what Jesus was capable of? Did he go running up to Andrew to offer his meager lunch for the crowds, insistent that his few little loaves be offered for the cause? He was not concerned with mathematics or proportions; he was concerned with giving what he had and watching what Jesus could do with it. His was a theology of abundance.

The difference of perspective in these three characters came from the choice of focal point. Andrew and Philip were focused on the inadequacy of their resources, particularly in light of the pressing needs before them. The boy was focused on the possibility that Jesus was getting ready to do something amazing, *even when what he had to work with wasn't enough.* The disciples suggested, "We'd better send them away to get food on their own because we sure don't have enough for them."[2] The boy wondered, "How are you going to do this with just two fish and five loaves, Mr. Jesus?"

I don't judge Philip and Andrew for focusing on the impossibility of the situation, but I do credit the boy with focusing on the possibility instead. He wasn't looking at the demands of the crowd as a comparison to what he had to offer in order to meet that demand. He was simply offering the little he had to Jesus. It wasn't enough, but he handed it over anyway.

For me, this passage holds a punch. I believe in the abundance of God, in the overflowing vessel of God's mercy and generosity. I believe in the unconditional love of God for each person ever created. The miracle of the loaves and fish isn't hard for me to accept; I have always believed that God feeds the hungry. But the miracle of the boy handing over his measly little lunch and thinking it might help a problem as big as the one on that hillside? That's a bit hard to take. What came into his mind to offer the little he had when clearly it was insufficient? He was not embarrassed by the inadequacy of his contribution; he was not ashamed of his own lack. He believed in the power of God to do something incredible with it. *That* is the kind of faith we need, the kind of faith I need. This perspective on abundance doesn't profess hope that what I have will

---

[2] See Mark 6:36 or Luke 9:12.

be enough if I just give it to God; it professes belief that *God is enough,* and it is God's abundance that must be relied upon.

What we have to offer may never be enough, but whoever said that it had to be? Certainly not God. God knows exactly what we have to offer because the only things we have to offer came from God in the first place. God does not scorn our inadequacy nor our shortcomings; God waits for us to surrender them to a much greater purpose than we could ever ask or imagine.

I remember hearing a parable of sorts once. A woman had died and found herself standing before the throne of God. God sat at his desk with a tapestry in front of him that represented the woman's life. He indicated to her that they would look together at the entirety of her existence from conception until death, and then he would tell her what her eternal destiny was to be. God started at the far-left side of the tapestry and asked her to narrate the different seasons of her life as she saw them reflected in the tapestry, reliving chronologically all the years of her life.

At first, it looked OK. Vibrant hues, a variety of beautiful patterns throughout her childhood, weavings and textures and designs that were both colorful and playful. Then, through her teen years, the tangles started to show up, gnarly dark spots mixed in with the smoother, prettier patches. As she continued through the first half of her life, she became embarrassed by the knots and the discolorations. Threads would be mangled and tied off before their pattern finished. In fact, there didn't seem to be a pattern at all, just random strings and stitches with an occasional splash of color. Somewhere in the middle, she found the day of the worst mistake of her life. It was a gaping hole right in the center of the weave. As she remembered the experience, shame washed over her and she could barely breathe, realizing that she could not hide it from God's gaze. She stumbled tearfully through the remaining years, seeing the mess that represented her life. Reaching the end, the woman started to tremble at first but then found herself weeping, her body wracked with the sobs that expressed her guilt, her remorse, and her shame. Finally, she said to God, "I am so sorry. I am so, so sorry for the mess I have made of the life you gave me. You gave me so much and look what I did with it. I have so little to show for it." She perceived that she had nothing worthwhile to offer at the very moment that mattered the most. Standing there before God at the end of her life, she was convinced of her own imminent damnation. What would God do with this paltry offering?

Ever so gently, God responded, "Hmm. It does look messy to you, doesn't it? Maybe you should come around and look at it from over here." The woman stood and walked over to God's side of the desk. She found herself looking at the most beautiful tapestry she had ever seen, a mix of light and dark, rough and smooth, patterned and spontaneous, with the design flowing out of the circular center of the weave with incredible intricacy. The image before her was stunning in its variety, unique and breathtaking. The mess she had perceived was the back side of this tapestry that she now gazed upon from God's perspective.

"It looks different from my side, doesn't it?" God said.

It is so easy, so frightfully *common*, to become overwhelmed with our mess, with our scarcity, to see things only "from our side." It is, after all, simple mathematics. Knots do not make for beautiful tapestries. Five loaves cannot feed five thousand people. One slingshot and a stone cannot take down a giant.[3] An elderly nomad cannot become the father of nations.[4] An infant born into a poor Jewish family cannot redeem the entirety of the human race. But somehow, all these things *did happen*. The math didn't hold up. The logic failed. God prevailed—

---

[3] See 1 Samuel 17:49, when David slays the Philistine Goliath with one single release of his slingshot.

[4] This is the promise of God to Abraham: "No longer will you be called Abram; your name will be Abraham, for I am making you the father of a multitude of nations" (Gen 17:5).

against all odds. God's point of view will always show for us—brilliantly, shockingly—the potential and the abundance.

How do we live out of *this* perspective, out of the theology of abundance? We learn from our loaves-and-fish friend to hand over the little we have to the power of the one who can do more than we could ever imagine. This young man proved himself a more faith-filled disciple than any of the Twelve gathered on the hillside that day. He was willing to hand over what he had, knowing it was nowhere near enough, without reproving himself for his inadequacy nor apologizing for being unable to feed the multitudes. He fixed his eyes on Jesus, waiting to see what God would do. In that act of trust, focused not on his own deficiency but on the possibilities of God, the miracle emerged—not despite his inadequacy but because of it.

Not one of us holds all the personal gifts or attributes that we wish we had. Sometimes we don't even have the gifts or attributes that we *need* for what life deals us. But we *do* have the gifts that we have, and what we have is enough, despite what we wish, despite what we think we need. It is enough because God is enough. And what we give back to God from ourselves will always be enough for God to work with. *But we must hand it over.*

What does this look like on a practical level? Since most of us won't be attending hillside functions with the Son of God anytime soon, I doubt we need to worry about feeding multitudes with our measly little lunches. But what about the contexts of our own lives? What about when someone I treasure is questioning her lovableness and I have tried everything to convince her of her worth, to no avail? What about when addiction ravages our most intimate relationships and we are powerless to do anything about it? What about when tragedy strikes and the faith I have long professed suddenly feels shaky and fragile? "Not enough" doesn't feel hopeful in circumstances such as this, and it is easy to wish we had more wisdom, more power, more *anything*.

When I was preparing to go to Taiwan as a missionary, I attended a month-long formation workshop in Maryknoll, New York. The purpose was to help us prepare for immersion in a different cultural reality from our own, but it was also to address the personal biases and attitudinal defaults that impacted our behaviors and perspectives. I learned much during those few weeks of class and conversation, but mostly I learned how much more I needed to learn. I learned that having little to give was not necessarily a bad thing. One story has forever changed how I think about what it means to have "enough."

An American missionary in Uganda was talking with some of her neighbors one morning as they were walking into the village. When asked why she was going into town, she told them that she needed to go to the library to use the computer and get on the internet. After marveling together about the wonders of the World Wide Web (which was still something of a novelty at that point), one of the women asked her if she was taking that long walk into town just to use the internet. She replied with a yes but explained it was because she needed to order a birthday gift for her daughter who was turning ten the following month. Oh, the joy that erupted in the small band of women walking together, rejoicing over the gift of life and already beginning to anticipate the birthday celebration of their young friend!

One in the group asked, "So what gift will you get to celebrate your daughter's life?"

The American missionary responded, "I want to get her a blue sweater that she can wear for our evening prayer meetings."

There was silence from the rest of the women for several minutes. The American wondered if she had said something wrong since the lack of response felt awkward. She hesitatingly asked, "Don't you think that's a nice gift?"

Finally, one of the Ugandan women said gently, "Emily already has a sweater. Or has it become ruined?"

"Do you mean the pink one?" asked the American.

"No, I saw her just yesterday wearing a beautiful black sweater."

"Oh, yes, yes, she has a black one, too. No, it isn't ruined, it's just that blue is her favorite color and it's her birthday and she doesn't have . . . a . . . blue . . ." The rest of the sentence trailed off as the American missionary felt the impact of her friends' queries. How many sweaters would be needed before it was "enough"?

In our Maryknoll preparation, this story became the catalyst for a lengthy conversation among us soon-to-be-missioned-across-the-sea disciples. We talked about materialism and fashion and consumerism and celebration. We talked about ethics and judgment and family and culture. We talked about poverty and privilege. But more than anything else, we talked about how much is "enough." Can "enough" become "what I have?" And how might the insatiability of "not enough" be addressed?[5]

If I don't think I have enough of something, whether material or immaterial, can I hand over the little that I do have? Can I ask God to bless it into enough? It might not be much, but if I am willing to hand it over, *in its entirety*, it just might "feed thousands." It just might become that which nourishes and sustains for the long haul. I might not have enough faith to make it through this awful tragedy, but can I give God the little faith I have? I might not have enough forgiveness toward the addict in our family, but can I hand over to God the little forgiveness I have? I might not have the right words to comfort my heartbroken friend, but can I give the words I do have, owning their insufficiency?

---

[5] To be clear, the issue of inadequacy of basic human needs—food, clean water, appropriate shelter, health care, education—is not the question here. Providing for the needs of all people to have "enough" in these realms is the responsibility of each one of us.

When we are feeling deficient or lacking, wouldn't we do well to pray to the anonymous "loaves and fishes" boy? Wouldn't we do well to ask his intercession when we feel we don't have enough wisdom or courage or hope? Wouldn't this young boy's surrender in the face of all things insufficient help us hand over our own inadequacies?

Nameless Child of the Multitude, continue to teach us. Teach us to focus on Christ and his ability to make miracles out of our lack. Teach us to focus on Jesus and the need he has for our offering of loaves and fish, meager as it might be. Teach us to focus on what is possible with God rather than what is impossible for us. Teach us to focus on God's greatness even while fully aware of our own smallness. Teach us to entrust all our shortages to God, allowing him to create sustenance out of our surrender.

Chapter 4: Stolen Mercies

A Gift from the Woman with a Hemorrhage

There was a woman afflicted with hemorrhages for twelve years. She had suffered greatly at the hands of many doctors and had spent all that she had. Yet she was not helped but only grew worse. She had heard about Jesus and came up behind him in the crowd and touched his cloak. She said, "If I but touch his clothes, I shall be cured." Immediately her flow of blood dried up. She felt in her body that she was healed of her affliction. Jesus, aware at once that power had gone out from him, turned around in the crowd and asked, "Who has touched my clothes?" But his disciples said to him, "You see how the crowd is pressing upon you, and yet you ask, 'Who touched me?'" And he looked around to see who had done it. The woman, realizing what had happened to her, approached in fear and trembling. She fell down before Jesus and told him the whole truth. He said to her, "Daughter, your faith has saved you. Go in peace and be cured of your affliction."

— *Mark 5:25-34*

℘

I stole something once. I was a kindergartener, and one afternoon after my grueling half day at school, I was with my mom at the grocery store up the street from our house. As I was standing in line, vaguely listening to my mom chat with Rose, the checker, I was longingly beholding the Ding Dongs and Milky Ways that were before me. (It's no coincidence that candy is at eye level to a kid when they're at the grocery store checkout.) I knew better than to ask for a whole candy bar, so instead my little six-year-old scheming brain imagined that my odds of success would be better if I set my sights on something less ambitious. I asked my mom if I could have one single Mary Jane candy, those incredible little butterscotch chews that cost only two cents. My mother could squeeze orange juice out of pennies, she pinched them so hard, so it came as no surprise that the answer to even this minimal request was no. As she emptied the cart onto the conveyor belt, I remained wistfully looking at the candy shelves. She wasn't paying any attention to me, trusting that her word alone was sufficient to end the discussion, so I took advantage of her distraction to simply pluck a single Mary Jane off the rack and put it in my jumper pocket. I waited until we got home to enjoy it, but as she was unpacking the groceries, she noticed that I was chewing on something.

"What are you eating?" my mother asked.

It may very well be that this type of moment is what the poets refer to as "the loss of innocence." I knew in my bones that I should tell the truth, but I also knew that the truth in this particular instance was not going to end well for me. *Do I choose the right thing or the self-serving thing?* As time froze, I could almost see the choice that lay before me; this was a moment of great import. Kohlberg's theory of moral development was being played out right there in our kitchen, and I was its unwitting agent.

I answered my mother, looking her right in the eye.

"Nothing," I said.

"What do you have in your mouth?"

Dang. The conversation hadn't just ended like I had hoped it would.

"A Mary Jane."

Maybe delayed virtue could erase original sin?

"Where did you get that?"

And there it was: the precise moment of truth. I don't remember deliberately choosing evil. I can't recall deciding to lie. I had just toyed with the truth, and it wasn't sufficient to release me from agony. What was a girl to do? I remember thinking that honesty in that moment would be an admission of doing something that I knew was wrong, that I had been told was forbidden. I was old enough to know better. Honesty would reveal to my mother that I was the kind of daughter I didn't want to be. If she knew I had taken the Mary Jane against her forbiddance, I would then be a daughter who defied her. I didn't want to be that kind of a daughter, so I thought I could trick her into believing I wasn't. The only problem was, I didn't yet have enough experience with dishonesty to know how to manipulate it. The best I could do in answer to her question was:

"I found it."

And *that* was the mistake. Stealing a two-cent piece of candy was one thing. Lying about it was quite another. The really funny part, from my now-adult point of view, is that I somehow considered my not-well-thought-out reply to have potential for appeasing my mother and allowing the curtain to close on the scene. What ensued was anything but that. The drama picked up quickly.

I'll spare you the details of the remainder of the event, but it involved spitting out the candy, replacing the lovely butterscotch flavor with a punitive Ivory soap tang, and marching back up to the grocery store for a confession that was infinitely more painful than anything I've ever experienced inside a church.

Suffice it to say that the lesson hit the mark: I never stole again, and I learned the importance of telling the whole truth, even when that truth might expose something unpleasant about myself to someone I love and respect. (As an adult I have come to realize that those "ugly truths" aren't invisible just because I don't own up to them. Denying them actually makes them uglier.)

What does this story have to do with the gospel passage at the start of this chapter? The woman with the hemorrhage from Mark's gospel account was trying to "steal" a bit of healing from Jesus. Just sneak in from behind, touch the hem of his garment, get yourself healed, and sneak back out. Jesus would never even have to know. This woman's faith was strong enough to believe that he could heal her, but her embarrassment about needing his help was too strong to be honest about it. So she decided to just take it instead of asking for it. After all, asking doctors for help had only made things worse— *for twelve years.* Who can blame her for wanting to just slink in and take something that she knew was available to her?

But when she made contact with Jesus' cloak, she got more than what she bargained for. The healing came instantaneously, but so did his awareness that someone had "taken" something from him, and he immediately started looking for her. My mother's "Where did you get that?" was a centuries-delayed echo of Jesus' question, "Who touched me?" Fear and trembling: the exact description of the response, both mine and hers.

This woman, our hemorrhaging friend, responded infinitely better to Jesus than I had to my mother, however. Mark tells us that, realizing what had happened, she told Jesus "the whole truth." She already had the cure, so conceivably she could have just disappeared into the crowd without anyone being the wiser. She could have absconded with the goods and left the scene. Instead, she opted for honesty and fuller connection, meeting his gaze and professing the faith that had elicited her healing, willing to deal with the consequences, come what may. And that choice gained for her so much more than renewed health; it gained for her a personal relationship with the very Son of God. He didn't just heal her; he *saw* her. And he called her "Daughter."

This poor woman suffered with her affliction for twelve years. Her suffering went well beyond the physical, as horrid as that would have been in and of itself. Mark tells us that she had suffered greatly "at the hands of many doctors" and that she had spent every penny she had on ineffective treatments. Beyond the physical suffering and mental anguish, however, her pain reached into religious and social realms as well. Her bleeding rendered her and anyone she touched ceremonially unclean according to Jewish custom. Not only was this woman unable to participate in religious ritual, but neither was anyone with whom she would have come in contact. She was taking an enormous risk even showing up in this kind of a crowd. If her affliction was discovered, she would be held in contempt for rendering so many others unclean and for putting them in danger. It seems that her desire to reach Jesus was stronger than her fear of the potential social, religious, or legal repercussions. She was in a desperate condition, she believed that Jesus could do what others could not, and she availed herself of an opportunity to receive what he had to give, even if she had to steal it.

It's ironic that she was made clean by touching Jesus. Touching him should have rendered *him* unclean, but instead it renders her *permanently cleaned*. Isn't it just like Jesus to turn the tables like that? The sick approach him, and rather than becoming infected by their illness, he purifies them of disease. Even those who witness the event are healthier for it. God's goodness overpowers every evil in its presence; God's mercy defeats every offense it encounters.

This woman's healing had already occurred, the power had already "gone out from" Jesus. So why did he seek out the one who had received it? There was no need for him to heal her; that had already been accomplished. He looked around to find the person who had been cured not to further heal her but to *see* her. For her part, she was afraid that she had been caught. Her fear did not prevent her from owning up to what she had done, though, and she approached him to make her admission. When the woman with the hemorrhage told Jesus "the whole truth" about touching him, he returned with an even larger truth: that the power of her affliction was defeated by the greater power of her faith in God's ability to heal her. She was not an undeserving woman; she was a beloved daughter. She only took what Jesus had already willingly given her. But she hadn't taken enough—she had not allowed herself to receive his loving gaze. Once she did, the gift was complete and she was able to leave—cured and named "Daughter."

The designation "Daughter" holds power when it is spoken in love. I have been extremely fortunate to have had parents who called me "Daughter" with love, but even so there were times I felt unloved and unlovable. At the age of seventy-two, my father was diagnosed with pancreatic cancer, a particularly unforgiving disease that ravaged his body for a brief but excruciating nine months before claiming his life. At the time, I was living in Connecticut, a thousand miles distant from him in St. Louis. My mom and siblings kept me informed about his health and promised to let me know when his final decline was beginning so I could make it home in time to say goodbye. That call came in the middle of the first semester of my senior year of college. I dropped everything and made it back home to be with him in his last week of life.

Dad was in the hospital, sedated for the pain of the tumor that had encroached upon most of his internal organs. When I arrived, I decided to spend nights with him to both keep him company and let my mom get some sleep at home. One night, I remember sitting at his bedside, holding his hand. It was clear that he didn't have much time left, and I knew there were some things I wanted to say to him. I had only been his daughter for twenty-three years—much too short a time, by my estimation, especially since I was an adolescent for several of those years, and the two of us did not get along very well. We were so much alike that everything he did embarrassed me and everything I did confused him. I guess it was a fairly typical father–teenage daughter relationship, but I regretted that it would never mature past that.

As I sat there that night, I knew I needed to ask his forgiveness; I knew I wanted to receive the healing that would come through that admission. I wanted him to assure me that I was still his beloved daughter despite how undeserving I was of the title. Like the woman with the hemorrhage, I approached the conversation in fear and trembling. In her encounter with Jesus, she thought, "If I but touch his clothes, I shall be cured." In my moment, I thought, "If I can confess this to him before he dies, maybe I can be forgiven." With head bowed low, I sat by his bedside and cried through my apologies for all the times when I had not been the kind of daughter my dad deserved. I apologized for the times I had been embarrassed to admit that he was my dad when most people assumed he was my grandfather. I wept for the times I had so rudely expressed my disdain by using the classic teenage eye roll, for the times I had openly and unabashedly treated him poorly. I apologized for being angry and impatient, and for the times I had been unforgiving or unrepentant. I expressed remorse for the Sundays when I shushed his singing in church. And above all, I told him how sorry I was that I would not have an opportunity to make it all up to him.

When I finished, I couldn't even raise my eyes to look at him. I waited for his response, but nothing came. With a sense of distress, I realized he was probably asleep and that I would need to repeat this awful litany again the next day. After a few moments more of silence, I lifted my head, figuring I would just grab a tissue to blow my nose and resume my vigil as he slept. But he wasn't asleep. He was looking straight at me with a look that I will never forget for as long as I live. It wasn't the look of forgiveness I was longing for. It wasn't a look of mercy. It wasn't even understanding. But neither was it a look of anger or of hurt or disappointment or sadness. The look I saw on my dad's face was one of confusion. Total and utter confusion. When my eyes met his, he simply said, "I don't remember any of that."

Unadulterated mercy: there it was, right there holding my hand, looking me in the eye, and naming me "Daughter." That night, I saw the gaze of God in my father's eyes and I truly understood God's mercy for the first time. Mercy isn't the same as forgiveness. Forgiveness acknowledges the wrongdoing and consents to move beyond it. Mercy doesn't even remember the wrongdoing. Mercy remembers only love—and mercy smiles with her memories. Mercy says that we have always and only ever been a beloved son or daughter.

That night in the hospital, I touched the hem of God's garment and, without asking for it or even deserving it, the bleeding of all my guilt and shame had stopped—immediately. Stolen mercies. I needn't have tried to steal them; they were already mine. The affliction of guilt I had carried was healed in that instant at my dad's bedside. His mercy had been available to me even before I asked for it. There was no need to steal it nor to sneak in at the last minute and hope to get it without him noticing. I should have known from my friend with the hemorrhage that my role as daughter had never been compromised despite the extent of my uncleanness. She and I have something very precious in common: the very mercy we were attempting to steal was ours for the taking all along. The only thing necessary was to reach for it and allow the gaze of mercy to fall on us. This is true for each one of us, God's sons and daughters all. Our family is made up of faith-filled would-be thieves, daring to reach for that which has belonged to us from the very beginning.

When we feel so guilty, so desperate to receive that which we need but feel we don't deserve, let us remember to pray to our gospel friend: O woman, healed by your faith and reminded of your name "Daughter," be forever and always our sister, emboldening us to reach out for God's mercy, that we might learn in so doing that it has been ours all along, we who are loved beyond all imagining.

Oh, and remember the story about the Mary Jane candy I stole as a kid? Well, here's what happened when I got back to the grocery store to confess to Rose, the checker. With quavering chin and tearful eyes, I confessed to her that I had taken a Mary Jane and I would pay her back double for it—all four cents at once. She looked down on me, such a sad, guilty little tyke, with a look of both affection and regret. Then, she picked up a bowl next to the register and said, "Oh, hon, didn't you ever see this li'l dish of candies I've got right here? I keep it on the counter for sweet little things like you. You can help yourself to a piece any time you come through my checkout. You just might have to stand on your tippy-toes to see it."

That which I had stealthily pilfered had been within my reach all along, completely free for the taking, just barely out of my line of sight. And isn't that revelation the exact gift given us by our friend, the woman with the hemorrhage?

As Rose took my four precious pennies, she also tilted the bowl toward me.

"You want a Life Saver?"

A Life Saver? Why, yes. Yes, that's exactly what I want.

Chapter 5: Wholeness Within

A Gift from the Man at the Pool in Bethesda

Now there is in Jerusalem at the Sheep [Gate] a pool called in Hebrew Bethesda, with five porticoes. In these lay a large number of ill, blind, lame, and crippled. One man was there who had been ill for thirty-eight years. When Jesus saw him lying there and knew that he had been ill for a long time, he said to him, "Do you want to be well?" The sick man answered him, "Sir, I have no one to put me into the pool when the water is stirred up; while I am on my way, someone else gets down there before me." Jesus said to him, "Rise, take up your mat, and walk." Immediately the man became well, took up his mat, and walked.

— John 5:2-9

૪ૐ

What a silly question, "Do you want to be well?" The poor guy had been sitting at the edge of a healing bath for thirty-eight years! The passage is clear: Jesus knew he had been sick for a long time, so why did he ask a question that had such an obvious answer? Well, maybe the answer isn't so obvious after all. Strangely, the man doesn't seem to answer Jesus' question; instead, his reply seems digressive, even a little self-pitying. Allow me to provide a personal interpretation, fanciful as it might be.

51

The response I hear from the man in this passage rings in my ears like this: "Do I want to be well? Hmmph. I've been here for the better part of the past four decades, buddy, and I have been waiting and waiting and waiting to be healed. But every time there's a possibility for me to get down into the water, someone else gets there first. Poor me. Poor, poor me."

Thirty-eight years is a long time to be sick. But it's an even longer time to be waiting. And it's a longer time yet to be complaining about how other people keep getting ahead of you. Think about where you were and what your life held thirty-eight years ago (or even just ten depending on your age!) It is my sincere hope that no one reading this book can say that you have spent three and a half decades sitting in the same spot, waiting for something good to happen to you, complaining when it didn't, and blaming others for the fact that it could have. Of course, it is possible that this could be someone's experience—it certainly did seem to be the experience of our sickly friend at the pool of Bethesda! Let's spend some time with him and his reality and see what we might learn from him, from his predicament, and from his encounter with Jesus.

In so many other stories depicting Jesus healing people, he touches them. Not so with this man. As a matter of fact, Jesus doesn't use the same verbiage with him that he does with so many others. He doesn't say, "Your faith has healed you," or, "Your sins are forgiven." He says, roughly, "Get up and get moving." In my imagination, I wonder about the tone of voice he used. Was it gentle, compassionate? I can imagine that. But what if it was more steely, annoyed? What if Jesus was trying to say, "Thirty-eight years, man. Really? You're telling me that for *thirty-eight* years (which adds up to more than 13,000 days, by the way) you have been sitting here whining that 'no one helps me' and 'someone else always beats me'? Have you *tried* walking? Have you even tested out whether or not you are able to stand up? Do you even want to be well? Listen, let's try something. Get up. Just get up. Thirty-eight years is too long. Let's not make it thirty-nine. Stand up, pick up your things, and go home."

And voilà, the gospel writer notes: he immediately became well, got up, and walked.

So what was the healing? Was it a physical healing, or was the illness of a different type? The Scripture does not specify this man's malady. He was lying among the blind, the lame, and the crippled, but all we know is that he had been "ill" for all those years. His own words seem to imply that along with the illness was a fair amount of self-pity. Jesus' question about whether or not he really wanted to be well is an important one, actually. Sometimes we become so comfortable in our patterns of victimhood and feeling sorry for ourselves that it's hard to even recognize that we've become immobilized, stuck in our gloom. A blunt question from someone who cares can jolt us out of our complacency and blindness: *do you even want life to be different?* It seems like such an obvious question with such an obvious answer, but is it? Oftentimes, questions like this evoke a defensive response. After all, who would ever *not* want an end to their misery?

An acquaintance of mine was in the throes of a very painful divorce a few years ago. In one of our conversations, she described to me her perspective on one aspect of her marriage. Her husband suffered from severe depression and anxiety and also had significant unresolved childhood trauma. She said, "We fight a lot, but sometimes we can go for long stretches when things seem fine. Then, just when I'm beginning to think we're going to be OK, all of a sudden he will *create* a crisis right out of thin air. He doesn't seem to know how to live comfortably in our relationship unless we are in crisis mode. It doesn't feel familiar or reliable to him, so he resorts to conflict, which feels more comfortable."

Granted, this is one side of a very complex relationship and clearly doesn't provide enough context to gauge the entirety of the situation, but as I listened to her, I couldn't help but think of the conversation between Jesus and the man at the pool of Bethesda. *Do you want to be well?* The question is not as straightforward as it might seem. Getting up and walking is hard work. And it can be scary, especially if we haven't done it for thirty-eight years.

Imagine if, in the scene at the pool in Bethesda, Jesus wasn't asking the question with annoyance, framing the man as a whiner like I did. Imagine if he was asking the question with extraordinary compassion, recognizing how paralyzing and confining life had become. Imagine Jesus looking at this man and *seeing* him. John writes that "Jesus saw him lying there and knew that he had been ill for a long time." I can imagine the feeling of heartbreak Jesus experienced over this man's prolonged illness—can't you feel it, too? I see Jesus squatting down to get to eye level with him, letting God's love reach him simply by looking at him pointedly. Could it be that the miraculous healing in this passage was simply Jesus revealing that the man already held the ability to walk within himself, that he just needed to conjure enough strength to summon it? What if the healing involved Jesus gently proposing that whatever ailed him needn't continue to paralyze or blind him, that it was his choice to claim the wholeness from within—and thus become well? Ever so gently, can't you hear Jesus say in a voice audible only to the man, "Rise, take up your mat, and walk. Get up, friend. It's time to go home." Can you imagine the sense of healing that would course through our Bethesda friend's veins simply because he had been seen, loved, and *empowered*? And finally, can you imagine the courage it would take for him, after thirty-eight years of waiting and aching, to try to stand?

The story is unambiguous: he became well *immediately.* And walked.

This is definitely a miracle story, but again, what exactly was the miracle? Maybe, just maybe, it was the man's realization after all those years of suffering that he had within himself all along the power to rise up. Maybe it just took thirty-eight years until Jesus came along and looked at him with healing love, validating his pain and inviting him back to himself. Perhaps Jesus' healing gaze resurrected in this man an inner power he had stopped believing existed.

Several years ago, I attended the funeral of a woman who was quite well known in the local Catholic community. I didn't know her personally, but during the course of her funeral Mass, a very strong resemblance to our Bethesda friend appeared.

I learned that Grace, the woman who had died, was a beloved mother, grandmother, friend, and wife. She was a woman in her early sixties who had just lost her two-year battle with breast cancer. Her husband and three daughters were the last to enter the church and were visibly devastated. Eight priests and a bishop had come to celebrate the final farewell of this woman. It quickly became obvious to me that Grace was one of those people you met and never forgot, a person whose character made an indelible mark on everyone she encountered, a woman who embodied her name in every way: *grace*. She was, quite clearly, beloved.

The priest who gave the homily had traveled over two thousand miles to bid her farewell, and he provided a stunning tribute to her selfless character. The prayers of the faithful highlighted the numerous charities that had benefited from her advocacy and faithful support. The remembrances were truly touching in every way, so through the first part of the funeral I had not yet made the connection between her and the man at the pool of Bethesda. This had not been a woman waiting for decades for someone *else* to do things. This had not been a woman who complained or wallowed in self-pity. This woman seemed to have been the very opposite of that—fully alive and doing all she could for the benefit of others.

But then came the eulogy, and I gained a whole new perspective on the woman who was called Grace. Her sister-in-law stood up and went on to give the following tribute:

On behalf of my brother Charles and his children, I would like to thank you for being here to celebrate Grace's life. It is true that she was a beautiful person, inside and out. She was generous, thoughtful, sensitive, and loving. But I am here to tell you something you might not know: she wasn't always like that.

As you know, Grace was my sister-in-law. When she and my brother were dating, I was not in favor of the match. She was a spoiled rotten brat and she complained about anything that didn't go her way. Yes, she was beautiful, but she was also what I considered a mollycoddled, too-big-for-her-britches sass. Charles was in love, dismissive of my complaints that Grace was shallow, self-centered, and seemingly only interested in him for his money. He would reprimand me gently, "You just don't know her the way I do. If you could see her through my eyes, you would love her too." Exasperated, I would usually end the argument by storming out of the room mumbling something about blinders and idiots.

When they got married, I tried to believe she would change and be "worthy" of my brother's love. Nope. Believe it or not, it actually got worse. She announced she didn't want to have children because she didn't want to wear those "horrid maternity clothes." She declared that she had no intention of getting a job. She spent her days at the mall and the spa ensuring that her appearance was, in her words, "On par with the rich and famous." Charles would come home from work to find her lying on the couch, exhausted after an arduous day of shopping and hairdressing. He would throw in a load of laundry and get dinner started while she finished her nails or soaked her feet.

After a year of this, I sat Charles down and begged him to open his eyes and see her for what she really was, a selfish woman who spent every dime he earned on her own selfish interests. I asked him to tell me one thing she had done that demonstrated that she genuinely loved him. He heard me out and responded calmly, "You just don't know her the way I do."

And he stood up and walked away. "Just one thing, tell me just one thing!" I shouted after him. I was heartbroken over the havoc my brother's naïveté was wreaking in his life. I actually kind of pitied him. If only he could just accept the truth, I thought. I prayed that God would give him eyes to see.

It turns out my prayer kind of boomeranged. Mine were the eyes that needed healing.

As the months went by, little by little things started to change. Charles would get home from work to find that the laundry had been started, or the plates were on the table. After a few months more, he would find that Grace had vacuumed the living room, or she would respond, "Oh, I didn't make it to any of the stores today," in answer to his question about where she had gone shopping. Charles told me that Grace even made cookies for the veterans at the VA hospital where he brought communion every Sunday. And then one week she started going with him.

Then, they had a baby girl. And another. And finally a third. As the years elapsed, little by little, painstakingly, Grace transformed into the woman every person in this church knew her to be: selfless, generous, and giving. She became the woman she had always been, hidden (at least to me) somewhere deep inside. Through love, she became, in every sense of the word, *grace embodied.*

Charles, you were right. You saw something in Grace that no one else would have guessed was there, and your love over these thirty-eight years allowed her to emerge as a gift for us all. Thank you for loving her into her best self and giving her to us. And Grace, thank you for teaching us that love makes it possible to become who we're meant to be. You have shown us how to let ourselves be seen and healed by someone who truly and wholly loves us, beyond all imagining.[1]

---

[1] I first told this story in the *Global Sisters Report* for the column on October 19, 2018. The original version can be found at https://www.globalsisters report.org/column/horizons/spirituality/being-loved-existence-55525.

It is delightfully coincidental to our gospel story that this couple, Grace and Charles, had been married for thirty-eight years, but the real resemblance between Grace and our Bethesda brother is the emergence of the restored beloved. Was Charles responsible for his wife's conversion? Yes and no. His love made the change possible, but Grace had to let herself be loved. Her conversion required her commitment to growth and, ultimately, transformation. Did Jesus heal the man who had been ill for thirty-eight years? Yes, but I wonder if that healing might also have required something in terms of cooperation.

Yes, Jesus had the power to heal the sick, and yes, Charles' love opened the possibilities for Grace to change. But Jesus did not heal the sick against their will. And Charles did not force Grace to be the woman he wanted. We must not forget the question posed at the pool of Bethesda: "Do you want to be well?" This question still lingers in the air, asked of each one of us today. Can we examine our own lives—what it is that has plagued us for years, causing us to look around and see how easy everyone else seems to have it, complaining and blaming them for our predicament? What pains your heart and your soul, paralyzing or blinding you to future possibilities? How might your hope be restored by an authentic look of love—and a belief in your ability to claim the wholeness within yourself? To what does your own inner grace call you today? Hear the gentle voice of God saying to you, as God looks directly into your eyes, *I see you. I know how long you've been hurting. Do you want to be healed? The wholeness lies within you. It's OK. Stand up. Pick yourself up. And walk. It's time to go home.*

Chapter 6: Remarkably Unremarkable

A Gift from the Shepherds Who Visit Jesus

In those days a decree went out from Caesar Augustus that the whole world should be enrolled. This was the first enrollment, when Quirinius was governor of Syria. So all went to be enrolled, each to his own town. And Joseph, too, went up from Galilee from the town of Nazareth to Judea, to the city of David that is called Bethlehem, because he was of the house and family of David, to be enrolled with Mary, his betrothed, who was with child. While they were there, the time came for her to have her child, and she gave birth to her firstborn son. She wrapped him in swaddling clothes and laid him in a manger, because there was no room for them in the inn.

Now there were shepherds in that region living in the fields and keeping the night watch over their flock. The angel of the Lord appeared to them and the glory of the Lord shone around them, and they were struck with great fear. The angel said to them, "Do not be afraid; for behold, I proclaim to you good news of great joy that will be for all the people. For today in the city of David a savior has been born for you who is Messiah and Lord. And this will be a sign for you: you will find an infant wrapped in swaddling clothes and lying in a manger." And suddenly there was a multitude of the heavenly host with the angel, praising God and saying:

"Glory to God in the highest
and on earth peace to those on whom his favor rests."

> When the angels went away from them to heaven, the shepherds said to one another, "Let us go, then, to Bethlehem to see this thing that has taken place, which the Lord has made known to us." So they went in haste and found Mary and Joseph, and the infant lying in the manger. When they saw this, they made known the message that had been told them about this child. All who heard it were amazed by what had been told them by the shepherds. And Mary kept all these things, reflecting on them in her heart. Then the shepherds returned, glorifying and praising God for all they had heard and seen, just as it had been told to them.

> — *Luke 2:1-20*

ℬ

Merry Christmas! It's hard to read this passage without envisioning the snow lightly falling, "Silent Night" gently playing, and a peaceful scene of shepherds, angels, and well-behaved barn animals sitting on display—and maybe even Linus saying, "Lights, please." Take a moment to gather together all those images as we look more closely at these verses.

Notice the proper names mentioned: Caesar Augustus, Quirinius, Joseph, Mary, even David. Then, the others: shepherds, angel, firstborn son. The angel has a proper role in the "multitude of the heavenly host," and in the next chapter we learn that the child is to be called Jesus, but nowhere are names given to the shepherds. No matter how carefully we inquire or how thoroughly we search, the names of the shepherds out in their fields that night have been lost.[1] And so it is here, at

---

[1] Interestingly, *The Book of the Bee*, a thirteenth-century source of biblical legends, claims there were seven shepherds and that their names were Asher, Zebulan, Justus, Nicodemus, Joseph, Barshabba, and Jose. See Metzger, "Names for the Nameless."

the story of his birth, that we first encounter the significance of insignificance in the life of Jesus. (Side note: My niece Megan was convinced as a child that one of the shepherds in the story was, in fact, a *shepherdess* named Gloria, since the angel in our household manger scene seemed to be putting a personalized "cloak" around the shepherd's shoulders. In reality, the angel was holding a banner emblazoned with the word *Gloria!* in reference to the song of the heavenly host indicated in verse 14. I never corrected Megan, and even now when I hear this passage read aloud at Christmastime, I envision a shepherdess named Gloria watching over her flock by night wearing a monogrammed jacket to shield her from the cold. Once I playfully proposed to Megan that maybe it was the *angel* who was named Gloria rather than the shepherd. She proceeded to tell me quite emphatically that, no, the shepherd's name was Gloria and the *angel's* name was Harold. You know, from the Christmas carol: "Hark! Harold the Angel Sings." I could never convince her that she had transposed the words from "Hark! The Herald Angels Sing!")

Regardless of what their actual historical names were, we read in Matthew's gospel that the night Jesus the Christ was born, these shepherds were tending their flocks as usual, experienced an angelic pronouncement, and hurriedly went to find the newborn child in Bethlehem. What must it have been like for them when they arrived, to be present at an event as momentous as the birth of the Christ? What must it have been like to have had a role in that storyline, among the few witnesses to an event that would change the entirety of human history? What must it have been like to have been chosen for such a part and yet to have your own name forgotten to history?

I grew up as the youngest of thirteen children, with twelve older siblings who had made names for themselves in school, in sports, in music, in drama, and in popularity. All throughout my childhood, I diligently kept track of how I was measuring up, particularly according to grade point average and pun delivery, two of the most prized personal attributes of our clan. As is likely often the case with younger siblings, I would frequently hear teachers say, "Oh, you're Joe's little sister," or, "Another Herbers! What musical instrument do you play?" This experience of being associated with the "bold and famous" and yet somehow still feeling anonymous is not uncommon. The ranks of such folks are quite large, including people trying to forge a new path outside the family business, children of famous actors or athletes, and spouses of high-ranking executives, to name just a few. Being a shepherd in the manger scene, next to the likes of the exotic King Melchior and his royal camel, Mary the Mother of God, and maybe even the angel Gabriel, can leave an anonymous shepherd feeling a little puny.

This kind of "puny shepherd syndrome" came to life for me one day during a homily when I was studying for my graduate degree. The theology school I attended undertook a search for a new president, and of the three candidates, two were Dominican priests living in the same community house: Fr. Rick and Fr. Dominic. Many of us, students and faculty alike, imagined that the sense of competition for the position caused a strain on their brotherly love in the house, but to their credit, nothing of the sort was evident in their words or affect (and believe me, I was paying attention for such indicators since I had a class with each of them). When the applications and interviews were completed and the announcement was made that Fr. Rick would be the next president of the institution, it just so happened that the homilist for the next day's liturgy was Fr. Dominic. The gospel passage was Jesus' teaching that "the last shall be first and the first shall be last." I remember sitting down for the sermon, thinking to myself, "Oh boy, this is either going to go really well or really, *really* not well." I braced for a homily that would be extremely awkward, extremely humble, or extremely short.

Fr. Dominic began in a dispassionate tone with this question: "What's it like to be cast in the Christmas play as the

Second Shepherd on the Right when the part you really wanted was Joseph?"

We all froze in place. He was approaching this thing head-on, apparently. "Extremely awkward" coming right up. I exchanged looks with a classmate, who winced and made the sign of the cross over herself. I closed my eyes as he began:

"Once a young child had been jubilant about his upcoming class Christmas play, wanting desperately to be cast as Jesus' foster father, Joseph. Instead, he came home with the role of Second Shepherd on the Right. Now, let's ask ourselves: What is the best way for a parent to speak to this child about what he is experiencing? What would be most helpful for both his emotional life and his character development?"

A congregation could not have been more uncomfortable, I am sure. No one responded. No one dared break eye contact, and I wished I had kept my eyes closed. My friend who had blessed herself in protection against the unpleasantries still had a wince upon her face, trying to brace herself for whatever was to come. Whether Fr. Dominic understood that waiting for a response to his question would fail to elicit one or that the uncomfortable silence in the room needed release, I'll never know, but he continued.

"A parent might want to comfort their tearful child with insistent reassurances that every part in the play is important and no one role is any more special than any other. A parent might justify that the Second Shepherd on the Right was the precise individual who was led by the angel to the stable and who was the first to see the newborn Jesus. A parent might promise that the costume worn by the Second Shepherd on the Right would be the most authentic, eye-catching costume on the stage opening night. A parent might even go so far as to turn their child's sights toward next year's play, when he could work harder to ensure getting the part of Joseph."

Some of us shifted uneasily in our seats. I remember thinking, "I have no idea how you are going to resolve the tension of this not-so-subtle analogy—or if you even want to—but please, oh please, just stop soon!" I honestly had no earthly idea how he could possibly salvage his dignity from what I perceived to be a very public display of unabashed resentment.

But then he said this:

"The truth is that the most honest and helpful thing a parent could say to that child is that his classmate cast as Joseph had more of what it took to be Joseph. Despite his wishes, the parent could add, he would simply need to acknowledge that there was someone in his class better suited to the role of Joseph. No two people have the same gifts, and the gifts of the boy's classmate are the ones that make for the better Joseph. There is no need to inflate the importance of the Second Shepherd on the Right. Talk to the child about what their gifts are, how to hone abilities and capitalize on talent, but do not appease the ego of the child with false praise or censure of his peer. Help him celebrate his friend who is Joseph. Help him celebrate right there from stage right, second shepherd."

I was more than stunned; I was dazzled. We all were—awed by the beauty of the homily and edified by the integrity of the homilist. In that brief sermon, we learned a lesson about the importance of unimportance that I have never forgotten. It's not about titles or fame, it seems. Our role in the life of God is about who we have been chosen to be and about being *that person* as fully as possible. We may not be named in the playbill; we may be one of many in the chorus. We may, in fact, be a simple shepherd—or shepherdess—who just happened to be in the right place at the right time to see angelic beings. But our presence in the life of God is neither random nor accidental. Our role has been written in purposely, and we must step up to play our part.

When I have a prayer intention that is really important to me, I have a particular set of go-to saints. You are likely familiar with the patron saints who get the most publicity: St. Anthony when you lose something, St. Francis when your pets are sick;

St. Christopher when you want to ask for safe travels, and St. Joseph when you need your house to sell (he comes with his own house-selling kit, by the way; if you don't believe me, look it up). And then there are the more sobering patrons: St. Peregrine for battling cancer; St. Therese of Lisieux and her rose novena; St. Michael, the archangel who does direct battle with evil. All of these are worthy intercessors, as are the newer saints: St. Gianna Beretta Molla, St. John Paul II, St. Oscar Romero. But these are not the saints I invoke when I have a really important personal prayer intention. When I am in need of the heavenly "big shots," I invoke the great company of anonymous saints. I call upon all those people who have lived quiet, normal, unremarkable lives but who have been good, good people. I invoke those folks who are in heaven celebrating life eternal with all the heavenly host but who themselves have never won a place in remembered history. Consider just for a moment how many of them there must be—century upon century and nation upon nation of people who led faith-filled, mundane lives and who now occupy heaven. Moms, grandpas, first responders, poets, migrant workers, blacksmiths, fishermen . . . the entirety of human history must be accounted for when we wonder how full heaven might be. These "forgotten saints" are just as surely heavenly residents as any of the great names we invoke so easily in our litanies—and there are *lots* of them.[2]

---

[2] I am indebted to my sister Joan for connecting this thought to the character Dorothea in Eliot's novel *Middlemarch*: "Her finely touched spirit had still its fine issues, though they were not widely visible. Her full nature, like that river of which Cyrus broke the strength, spent itself in channels which had no great name on the earth. But the effect of her being on those around her was incalculably diffusive: for the growing good of the world is partly dependent on unhistoric acts; and that things are not so ill with you and me as they might have been, is half owing to the number who lived faithfully a hidden life, and rest in unvisited tombs." George Eliot, *Middlemarch* (London: The Folio Society, 1999), 759.

I like to imagine them in heaven, doing whatever it is we do in heaven, getting that prayer request over some kind of celestial intercom like in *It's a Wonderful Life*: "Clarence, you're up. And Titanus, Lydica, Joo-chan, Melthus, Chidi, heck, everybody who isn't otherwise occupied, this one's for you guys." Then, the entire body of those stranger-saints, the full chorus of those beautifully unnamed and unknown-to-us saints, joins in communion to pray with and for whatever intention it is that I've raised up. *That* is a celestial intercession that rocks. (Not that any of them don't, but the sheer power of this image gets me every time. I also imagine them being just tickled pink to finally have a request for their help.) Such is my prayer in my most dire need, and I highly recommend it: O Nameless Saints of Eternity, come to my aid!

It works both ways, actually. When I was teaching high school theology, we would begin every class with a prayer, and I would always open it up to the students' intentions. Sometimes they used the prayer as a tool to stall the day's quiz or would feel the need to compete as if they were upping the ante in a poker game.

"For a special intention," the first student would say.

"For two special intentions and a situation," someone else would add.

"For a situation, a friend who's upset, and for a difficult relationship."

I would derail this quickly accelerating competition by collecting the remaining intentions with a summary statement: "For all those who need our prayer today, we pray to the Lord. Amen."

Usually, praying for others was a lovely way to begin the class and provided a sacred space to call to mind the very real and very important circumstances that weighed on our hearts. One day when I opened the prayer, Ashley, a senior theology student, said, "I want to pray for somebody who died . . ."

I didn't usually pry into the students' intentions, but the way she said it, with the sentence seeming incomplete, made me ask, "Do you want to say more, Ash?"

"Yeah. Well, no. I mean, maybe. I don't know anything else. I didn't know the guy. But . . ."

Mm-hmm, I thought. *Stall tactic.* I began to admonish her. "Ashley . . ."

"No, seriously. Let me explain," she insisted. "My brother and I were coming home last night from where we work and were hungry. It was around 9:30 and nothing was open. We looked for a Steak 'n Shake because, you know, they're always open, 24-7. So we pulled in and got out of the car, but when we got to the door, it was locked, and there was a sign that said, 'Closed due to a death in the family.' I just want to pray for that family and for whoever died."

I was transfixed by this young woman's sensitivity. Indeed, the insight she provided that day affected my life profoundly and permanently. She taught me this: the communion of saints works in both directions, from heaven to earth and from earth to heaven. Somewhere up there in heaven that day, the celestial intercom rang again. "Jimmy, can you come to the office, please? Look, we just got a prayer sent up here for your benefit. A girl by the name of Ashley. You know her?"

"Nope. Never met her."

"Well, she and about twenty of her friends just sent up a whole bunch of prayers for you."

"Really? You sure you have the right guy? I'm telling you, I don't know her."

"Yep, you're the guy. Family owns a Steak 'n Shake in Caseyville, right?"

"Yeah, that's right. Hmm. How about that. She doesn't even know me."

Or does she?

We needn't have big names or snazzy titles. Whether we're the Second Shepherd on the Right, that Steak 'n Shake guy from southern Illinois, or Gloria the misnamed shepherdess, we matter, and we are known. Our role—in the life of God and in the communion of saints—really matters. Nobody wants to be forgotten to history, especially salvation history, but the written histories in books and song are not the legacies that count. The legacy we leave in each other's lives is what will last. Additionally, we each have a legacy in the story of God. Every one of us plays a role in the life story of God, whether it is an exceptional one like Peter or a less-flashy one like Jimmy the Steak 'n Shake guy. What is important is that, whether you are one of the apostles or a simple field hand, the saint of Calcutta[3] or the Second Shepherd on the Right, each one of us in the communion of saints, unremarkable as we may be, has something in common: our names are written on the Heart of God. And *that* is remarkable.

---

[3] A reference to Mother Teresa; on September 5, 2017, the Vatican named Mother Teresa the patron saint of Kolkata (Calcutta), India.

Chapter 7: What About Us?

A Gift from the Crowds at Capernaum

> At sunset, all who had people sick with various diseases brought them to him. He laid his hands on each of them and cured them. And demons also came out from many, shouting, "You are the Son of God." But he rebuked them and did not allow them to speak because they knew that he was the Messiah.
>
> At daybreak, Jesus left and went to a deserted place. The crowds went looking for him, and when they came to him, they tried to prevent him from leaving them. But he said to them, "To the other towns also I must proclaim the good news of the kingdom of God, because for this purpose I have been sent." And he was preaching in the synagogues of Judea.
>
> — *Luke 4:40-44*

༄

Such a beautiful scene from the city of Capernaum: Jesus receives hordes of ailing people, and when he touches them, they are healed. "People sick with various diseases"—likely everything from leprosy to blindness to paralysis to demonic possession—all experience miracles at the hands of a caring God. What a joy for those individuals and their loved ones! But then Jesus leaves, saying that he's going to "other towns."

69

Judea and Galilee were not neighboring areas, so when Jesus leaves Capernaum in Galilee to go to the synagogues of Judea (at least a sixty-kilometer journey), he gives the impression that he might not return. Let's for a moment imagine the experience of all the folks who showed up with their sick loved ones the day *after* Jesus left. We may not have their names, but I am sure they existed, and I am certain they have something to teach us today.

"Where is he? What do you mean he's gone? Why? Where did he go? What 'other towns'? Will he be back? What about us?"

Disappointment doesn't even come close to describing the experience of these "day after" folks, I expect. The feelings might be more akin to desperation, anguish, hopelessness, anger, resentment. The mother carrying her dying child in her arms asks the question of her neighbor whose child was healed the previous day, "Why has he gone? How were you so fortunate and I am not? My son needs him, too!" The leper who had been healed brings to town his other four leprous friends, seeking Jesus and asking, "How can it be that he has gone? He was here yesterday—he healed me. I have brought these others with me today also to be touched by him." A blind man is led to the place Jesus had been and asks, "He is gone? What about the rest of us?" How many more must have come looking for Jesus after he had already departed? And how are we to reconcile the fact that they were not lucky enough to receive his gift of healing?

Luck—is that it? Good fortune? Or is it more about timing or karma? How are we to answer the question of why some people are healed and others aren't, not just then in the city of Capernaum but even now in our own towns, our own families? We have likely all heard stories about people who "should have been" in the Twin Towers on September 11, 2001, who weren't there that day for one reason or another. Maybe they called in sick to work, maybe their scheduled appointment was cancelled, or maybe they were just running late that morning. I have heard these experiences called a blessing, a miracle. But what about the people who *shouldn't* have been in the Twin Towers that day and yet were—people who came to work that morning to fill in for the one who had called in sick, or whose appointments were rescheduled to that date from a previous one, or who just happened to go in early that morning? If the first group of people are considered "blessed" and recipients of a miracle, what about the second group? There is no easy way to engage this conversation, for we know even before we begin that we will find no answers. We are left with only questions, and those questions are enough to break our hearts.

I'm not exactly a connoisseur of pop rock music, and any song that begins with the lyrics "La da da da da, la da da da da" doesn't exactly get my hopes up for having a life-altering message, but when I first encountered the song "What About Us," I heard in its words a familiar cry and listened carefully to the lyrics. I knew the experience being described. In this song, the artist P!nk expresses the feelings of the "we weren't supposed to be there" people at the World Trade Center and the "day after" crowds at Capernaum. The lyrics could be the articulation of any one of us who feels like we missed out on the types of miracles other people were fortunate enough to receive. The refrain can practically be heard coming from the mouths of "the crowd" at Capernaum as they learn of Jesus' departure:

What about us?

What about all the times you said you had the answers?

What about us?

What about all the broken happy ever afters?

What about us?

What about all the plans that ended in disaster?

What about love? What about trust? What about us?[1]

---

[1] P!nk, "What About Us," track 4 on *Beautiful Trauma*, RCA, 2017, MP3. Permission requested.

When tragedy strikes or when miracles don't happen, a sense of betrayal can set in. After all, isn't God supposed to be the one who takes care of us? Aren't we supposed to place our trust in the loving God who would never abandon his children? Isn't God the one who says, "I know well the plans I have in mind for you . . . plans for your welfare and not for woe, so as to give you a future of hope" (Jer 29:11)? How do we pray to this God when our happily ever afters have been shattered or when our plans end in disaster? In those times, aren't our prayers akin to P!nk's lyrics: *What about love? What about trust? What about us?*

Yes, God, what about that? What about that trust thing that you ask of us? What about that love thing that you promise us—unconditionally, unwaveringly, unstoppably? Where was your love when tragedy struck? What was the point of trusting you if you weren't going to help? Where were you? Where are you? Why won't you do something? Jesus, why did you leave Capernaum before you healed *everyone?* What, were you tired? Did some people matter more to you than others? Did you not *care?*

In the Gospel of Mark, the disciples put this very question to Jesus upon finding him asleep in the boat in the midst of a life-threatening storm at sea: "Teacher, do you not care that we are perishing?" they cry (Mark 4:38). When life's storms are raging all around us and we are in danger, finding Jesus "asleep in the boat" stirs up several emotions: First, outrage. Can you feel the emotion behind the question, "Do you not care?" *Jesus, do you not care that we are perishing, that we are afraid? How can you be inattentive?* Second, fear or maybe even dread. What does it mean for me if indeed God does not care? Can anything be relied upon if not that? What am I to do and where am I to turn if God cannot be trusted? *What about love? What about trust? What about us?*

In my lifetime, I have listened to stories of people overwhelmed with gratitude for the miraculous recovery of their loved ones from life-threatening illnesses. I have likewise listened to stories of people who are overwhelmed with grief or rage over the inexplicable death of a loved one. Even as I write this chapter, I am in conversation with two different individuals, one who has just buried her sister after a freak car accident and the other who is bringing her father home from the hospital after an equally freaky medical mishap that almost killed him. The questions from P!nk's song resound in our very souls as we rail against the inconsistencies of God's healings. Is it really just that we were a day late to Capernaum and that we missed our chance to benefit from God's healing touch? In the end, is our life in God really only happenstance?

The entirety of the human race is currently in the midst of the COVID-19 pandemic. Every living person is threatened by this illness ravaging the globe. Some have gotten sick and recovered; others have gotten sick and died, with identical treatments producing varying results. Additionally, natural disasters strike with impunity, seeming to destroy the most vulnerable communities again and again by wind, water, or fire. Bad things happen to good people, and sometimes greed and manipulation prove more effective than kindness and generosity as techniques for success. If following God faithfully, believing in God's goodness and providence, and committing to a life of virtue doesn't earn us any advantage in the realm of tragedy and heartbreak, then what's the point?

The question of theodicy has always plagued us: Why does evil exist? How can a good God allow bad things to happen—doesn't that mean God is either not all-good because he allows evil or not all-powerful because he cannot prevent it? Why didn't Jesus cure blindness itself rather than just heal a few random blind people? Why didn't he *eradicate* sickness, demonic possession, and evil once and for all?

Clearly, answers to these questions are elusive; the purpose of raising them in this chapter is not to provide answers. Rather, the question "What about us?" is asked in order to hear it echoed through the ages, not just on the tongues of the nameless individuals in the city of Capernaum at the time of Jesus, but also as it has risen up from thousands of their ancestors in the two millennia since. Indeed, the cry rises up still today.

I've never been a proponent of the saying "If it happened, it must be God's will" or even "Everything happens for a reason." I recognize that these perspectives give many people great comfort, so I do not intend to negate their positive impact on anyone else's faith and spirituality. I have found, however, that when I am looking for words to speak to someone experiencing tragedy, neither one of these two statements helps much, and they actually sound hollow even to my own ears. I simply cannot look into the eyes of a parent who has just lost a child and make a statement implying that God willed the child to die, nor can I stomach the thought that our God would have a "reason" to plunge that family into grief. What I do believe with all my heart and soul, however, is that God can take the worst of what life presents—tragedy, violence, even sin—and transform it into something else, something good. I believe that if we can traverse the agonizing terrain of pain, sorrow, and doubt, we will come out on the other side of it. The Christian story is based on this belief. We are a resurrection people, believing that every Good Friday will lead to an Easter Sunday, that every tomb will be emptied, that death is not the last word. The life, crucifixion, and resurrection of Jesus didn't end suffering and death once and for all, but it did rob those realities of their finality and drain them of their ultimate victory.

Looking into the eyes of grieving parents, I can't say, "This is for the best," or, "God must want it this way." I can only say, "This must be awful. But you are not alone. You can get through this, awful as it is. Heartbrokenness is evidence of love outpoured. I'm so sorry love hurts so much right now." When we weep because of love, love weeps with us. And love's name is God.

The nameless crowds who showed up in Capernaum the day after Jesus left likely asked lots of questions, both out loud and to themselves. As they returned home, still sick or lame or impaired, how did their belief in Jesus fare? What was their prayer to God that night? Was it more cautious? Were they still able to praise and thank God? What was the quality of their trust? These are not questions for the Galileans only; these are our questions, too.

At a wake recently, I overheard the most beautiful example of this type of faith in a conversation between a mother and her eight-year-old daughter. The woman who had died was the godmother of the child, and apparently the two of them spent every Thursday afternoon together, sometimes shopping, sometimes doing homework, sometimes cooking. The child had been suddenly and cruelly robbed of a lifetime more of Thursdays, and she was devastated as a result.

"I am so sad," said the child, leaning her head against her mother's shoulder.

"I know," comforted her mother, also grief-stricken at the tragic loss of her friend.

"Why did God let this happen?" asked the child.

"I don't know, honey," said the mother.

"I'm mad at God for letting her die."

"Me too."

There were a few moments of silence. Then, the girl said through tears, "I don't know if I can get through this."

The mother was also crying. She said, "I feel the same way. But I'll tell you what I do know. I know that there's only one way to try to get through this. We get through this *together*."

Together. We get through this together.

The Hiding Place is a book written by Corrie ten Boom in 1971.[2] She relates her experiences, first in Holland helping to hide Jews, and then in Nazi concentration camps where she

---

[2] Corrie ten Boom, *The Hiding Place* (New York: Bantam, 1971).

and her sister Betsie endured unspeakable hardships during the Second World War. The sisters' Christian faith buoyed them and their fellow prisoners through the horrific days, but Corrie had trouble with Betsie's prayer at one point in the story. Having been transferred to a barracks that was flea-infested, Betsie insisted that they remain faithful to the prayer of the Bible, to "[i]n all circumstances give thanks" (1 Thess 5:18) by offering a prayer of thanksgiving for the fleas. This was altogether too much for Corrie to bear, and she was certain that Betsie's perspective was wrongheaded this time. "How could a vermin-ridden dormitory possibly be the stuff of gratitude? How could God be doing something good in such a revolting reality?" Corrie thought. (Betsie might be the saint in the story, but Corrie has always been my soul sister.) During their time in Barracks 28 at Ravensbruck, one of the most notorious of the Nazi concentration camps, Betsie and Corrie formed prayer groups among the women. Although Corrie was confused by the guards' lax supervision of the barracks, she and Betsie were delighted to be able to form two groups for nightly faith sharing without fear of discovery. After several weeks, Betsie overheard one of the guards explaining why he refused to enter Barracks 28: "That place is crawling with fleas!"[3] It was then that Corrie realized the value of Betsie's instinct to pray in thanksgiving, even for blessings that hadn't yet emerged. Betsie held an unwavering trust that God would "easter" even fleas into something grace-filled and beautiful, and that is exactly what God did.[4]

It is one thing to say God brought something life-giving even out of the atrocities of a Nazi concentration camp; it is

---

[3] ten Boom, *Hiding Place*, 209.

[4] I am taking some liberties in using "easter" as a verb. My meaning is to recognize that the transformative power demonstrated on Easter in the resurrection of Jesus is not limited to that singular Sunday morning but in fact is repeated every time God brings beauty after pain, life after destruction, or hope after disaster.

quite another to say that God willed those atrocities.[5] Did God desire such evil? Did God the Father want humanity to reject, scorn, and crucify his Son? Or does God allow each of us to exercise our free will, knowing that when it results in evil or suffering, God will create something new out of it, will easter it into new life? This is the question on which the Christian faith relies. This is the question that can only be answered from within a relationship of trust.

Trust like this is heroic. I have been inspired by people in my own life who have exhibited it. We have everyday heroes right in our midst. These are the people who, in their very real, very difficult circumstances—whether that means fleas, illness, tragedy, or any other variety of hardship—still believe that God is big enough, powerful enough, and loving enough to stay with them, to endure with them, and to see them through to the other side of the darkness. It's not a flashy kind of faith, this trust-in-the-between-times faith. It is the faith that sits through Holy Saturday, certain only of the horror of Good Friday but believing that there must be something else coming simply because God promised. It is the faith that knows the sun shines behind every cloud, even if it doesn't shine on our faces today. It is the faith that knows that even if Jesus has left Capernaum without healing us, he is still our Messiah. It is the faith that believes that, yes, God *does care* if we are perishing, for God is in the boat with us.

---

[5] A theological distinction is in order. The *Catechism of the Catholic Church* instructs about the *permissive will of God*: "God is in no way, directly or indirectly, the cause of moral evil. He permits it, however, because he respects the freedom of his creatures [even to choose evil] and, mysteriously, knows how to derive good from it. 'For almighty God . . ., because he is supremely good, would never allow any evil whatsoever to exist in his works if he were not so all-powerful and good as to cause good to emerge from evil itself.' [St. Augustine, *Enchiridion* 3, 11: PL 40, 236.]" *Catechism of the Catholic Church*, 2nd ed. (Washington, DC: United States Catholic Conference—Libreria Editrice Vaticana, 1997), 311.

The question "What about us?" is a question asked when we feel we have been neglected, abandoned. It comes out of a place of hurt and need. Perhaps, as our voices join the chorus of our "day late" Capernaum brothers and sisters, we might dare to hear this response to the question emerging out of our heartbrokenness:

Yes, my love, what about us? The "us" to which you refer is not me having left you; "us" includes me. You and I are ever one. We are in this together, and we will get through this together. I may seem far distant, it may even seem to you that I have left you, but I have not. I cannot. I have gone to prepare a place for you, and when I return, I will bring you with me, that where I am you shall also be. My experience will be yours—not just in its pain but also in its glory. What about us, you ask? It has always been and will always be all about us. It's about love. It's about trust. It's about us.

Chapter 8: It's Not Fair

A Gift from the Crucified Thief

When they came to the place called the Skull, they crucified [Jesus] and the criminals there, one on his right, the other on his left.

Above him there was an inscription that read, "This is the King of the Jews."

Now one of the criminals hanging there reviled Jesus, saying, "Are you not the Messiah? Save yourself and us." The other, however, rebuking him, said in reply, "Have you no fear of God, for you are subject to the same condemnation? And indeed, we have been condemned justly, for the sentence we received corresponds to our crimes, but this man has done nothing criminal." Then he said, "Jesus, remember me when you come into your kingdom." He replied to him, "Amen, I say to you, today you will be with me in Paradise."

— *Luke 23:33, 38-43*

Not the easiest passage from Scripture, this one depicting the gruesome death scene of our Savior. Yet there is something beautifully touching about the verbal exchange on Calvary between Jesus and the subject of this chapter's nameless gospel friend, the "good thief."[1] The other criminal's taunting sets a striking counterpoint to the faith professed by this convict who is soon to be in paradise alongside Jesus. The content and *feel* of their conversation always seems somewhat peculiar to me when I picture the three of them hanging there dying that day: two men flanking Jesus, guilty in their sentence and paying for their crimes, and Jesus in the center, innocent in his sentence and paying for *our* crimes.

One of the convicts resorts to taunting and ridicule with his last breaths. Really? What a horribly tragic way to leave life, feeling angry and spiteful. But the other convict nears his end with a perspective of compassion and trust. He admits his guilt while simultaneously professing faith in Jesus, a faith tinged with hope. He has hope that, despite his guilt, Jesus might "put in a good word" for him in the kingdom. I find the attitude of this faith-filled felon breathtaking for three reasons: he truly recognized who Jesus was, he genuinely understood the kingdom of God, and he knew that he would be welcomed there. How did he know that? From where did his certitude come?

Just imagine if he reached paradise before Jesus did that day. *Knock, knock, knock* on the gates of heaven. Father God answers, opening the door to find a grungy, mangled man on the step.

"Yes?" Father God inquires warily.

"Hi. Is Jesus here?" asks the good thief.

"No, he hasn't been here for quite some time. We aren't open for business," states God.

"Well, he told me to meet him here today. This is paradise, right?"

---

[1] The fourth-century text entitled the *Gospel of Nicodemus* provides us with the names Dysmas for this good thief and Gestas for the other criminal. Other sources name the pair Zoatham and Camma or Joathas and Maggatras. Luke only tells us that the good thief is one of two criminals crucified alongside Jesus that day. See Metzger, "Names for the Nameless."

"Yes," answers God. "Hey, aren't you one of the guys with him on Calvary this morning? You're one of the convicted criminals sentenced to death, correct?"

"Yes," mutters the good thief, suddenly ashamed.

"And my Son told you that you were welcome here?" asks God.

Mumbling: "I thought that's what he said . . ."

With a wide grin breaking over his face, Father God then roars gleefully: "Yep, that sounds about right. Come on in, we've got a lot to do before everyone else starts arriving! If you're any indication, he's been fruitful in his mission and it's going to be quite a crowd. That's my boy!"

So are we to understand from the encounter on Calvary between Jesus and the thief-turned-believer that in the end, no matter what we've done, how much havoc we've wreaked in our own lives or in the lives of others, so long as we profess faith in God we will be welcomed into heaven, no questions asked? On one hand, that is such a beautiful and consoling thought, that our worst mistakes or our biggest sins cannot define us permanently, that God's mercy will always be bigger than our screwups. But on the other hand, this notion of last-minute redemption leaves me feeling somewhat like there's no point in trying to "be good." If anybody can just slide in at the last moment with a deathbed conversion, why not live it up while we can and just say "sorry" at the end?[2]

It is a difficult question, this one that struggles to understand the relationship between God's mercy and God's justice. It is not a new question; indeed, it's an ancient one. It is the quandary of why God chose Abel instead of Cain; Jacob rather than Esau; Moses and David, murderers both. The genealogy

---

[2] St. Augustine, one of the greatest saints of the early church, uttered a prayer in his younger days according to this very sentiment: "Lord, grant me chastity and continence, but not yet." Augustine of Hippo, *Confessions*, Book 8, Chapter 7, trans. R. S. Pine-Coffin (London: Penguin, 1961), 169.

of the Messiah is filled with substantially flawed personages—
and this simultaneously comforts and confounds me. God's
clemency is something upon which we all must rely, of course,
but is it something to which any of us is entitled? Can we assume
that no matter what the quality of our character throughout
the duration of our life, as long as we make one solid profes-
sion of faith at the end we'll sail right through to our eternal
happiness? Something about that just doesn't sit right, doesn't
seem all that *fair*. And as a product of Western culture, German-
Irish upbringing, Catholic social teaching, and a very large
family, I hold "fair" to be an extraordinarily strong value.[3]

We could probably all tell stories about experiences where
we were the victims of something unfair—and as we call those
moments to mind, I imagine that the injustice of it "gets our
goat" all over again. Likewise, I imagine we could tell stories
of when we were the beneficiaries of an undeserved recognition or reward, but these memories probably evoke something
more akin to sheepishness. Fairness, it seems, is a sticky wicket.
When the statement "That's not fair!" is made, our emotional
response is likely conditioned by our loyalties to the parties
involved or the issue at hand. When it's about sizes of pie
servings, I might shrug it off as unimportant (depending on
how much I like pie.) When it's about a flag on the play in
overtime, I might insist on review. When it's about systemic
racism, I might feel galvanized to advocate for genuine transformative change. When it's about leniency granted in a court
sentence, I might . . . well, my response depends on whether
I'm associated with the victim or the perpetrator of the crime
in question.

Let me propose a few questions: What happens when we
witness someone getting an honor they don't deserve? Do we
find something irksome about the "bad actors" who end up

---

[3] It is worth noting that the value of fairness varies according to culture
and should not be generalized as universally important.

with the same place in heaven as those who have spent their whole lives being good? For as poetic as the story of the good thief is, is there a part of us that resents the lack of proportionality between his lifelong behavior and his eternal reward?

If your response to even one of these questions is any variation on the emotion "miffed," you are in good company. An expression of displeasure to such situations appears more than once in Scripture, particularly in the gospels. As a matter of fact, two parables of Jesus—the parable of the prodigal son[4] and the parable of the workers in the vineyard[5]—speak directly to this feeling. Most of us, I would venture to say, have at least a little sympathy for the complaint of the older brother of the prodigal son. He protests his father's extravagant celebration when his brother returns from months of debauchery: "Look, all these years I served you and not once did I disobey your orders; yet you never gave me even a young goat to feast on with my friends" (Luke 15:29). Sounds a lot like "It's not fair!" doesn't it? Likewise, we also might share the sentiments of the workers who had been hired by the vineyard owner at the start of the day when they received the same wage as those hired at the end of the day: "These last ones worked only one hour, and you have made them equal to us, who bore the day's burden and the heat" (Matt 20:12). Yet another iteration of "It's not fair!"

These two parables from Jesus set the stage for what happens at "the place called the Skull" on the day of crucifixion. It would be both untrue and unwise to claim that Jesus didn't care about fairness. He cared passionately that all people received what they deserved—specifically, an unimpeded relationship with God. Anything that mitigated against that fundamental entitlement Jesus deemed unfair. Beyond that, things got fuzzy. Consider this:

---

[4] See Luke 15:11-32.
[5] See Matthew 20:1-16.

Three guys walk into a bar: a thief, a prodigal son, and a late worker in the vineyard. The thief says to the prodigal son, "Wow, you must be having a lot of fun with your share of the inheritance. Parties, good times, no responsibilities. Livin' the dream, brother, right?"

The prodigal snorts. "Huh, yeah. But no. Sure, it was fun in the beginning, feeling free and unbound. But that gets old really fast, you know? And I'm starting to wonder why I ever left my dad in the first place. He is the best man I know. Leaving his house was the worst decision of my life. I'm actually thinking of reclaiming my real inheritance—being his son. I wouldn't care two jots if I had to work as a field hand for him, as long as I could get him back as my father."

With a scoff, the thief turns to the vineyard worker. "How about you, then? Such a deal, getting a full day's wage for only working an hour. Talk about a dream—none of the work and all of the benefits!"

"No, brother," says the vineyard worker. "Sure, I can understand why the guys who had been out there all day felt like I didn't deserve the pay. I didn't. But honestly, that vineyard owner, that man who hired me so late in the day? I would work for that guy for free. He's the best man I know. I'm just sorry I haven't been working for him all along. His full-time employees, they're the ones with the real wealth. I wish I had known him for as long as they have."

After a few moments of silence, the thief mutters to himself, "The kingdom of God is like a vineyard owner . . . the kingdom of God is like a father with two sons . . . the kingdom of God . . . seems like a curious place inhabited by curious folk . . ." He walks out of the bar and right into the Roman authorities, who jail him, prosecute him, and condemn him to death by crucifixion. The next day he is led to the place of the Skull, crucified together with two others—his partner in crime and a man named Jesus who speaks about the kingdom of God—*his kingdom*. It sounds very familiar. The thief remembers the story about the vineyard owner, the story about the prodigal's father, and he understands that the Jesus beside him resembles both. He begins to hope for his own future, not to escape death but to escape damnation.

And this is how an everyday thief becomes a good thief— by recognizing that the real prize is not getting away with a life of indulgence or laziness or criminality. The real prize is the kingdom, home to the God who would love even the indulgent, the lazy, and the criminal. And the more opportunity we have to spend with that God in that kingdom—whether it be in eternity or in the kingdom come right now—the richer our life is.

If we were to entertain a conversation with the good thief about his experience at the place of the Skull, it might go something like this:

"So was it just one mistake that got you crucified or was criminal stuff more habitual for you?" we ask.

The good thief responds, "I'm sorry to say it was a lot more than one mistake. That other guy hanging at the Skull with Jesus and me? He and I were partners in crime, literally. Those snide remarks of his could just as well have come from my mouth. To tell you the truth, I'm not sure what changed. I guess it was realizing that I really was going to die. As I hung there and paid attention to Jesus—how he prayed through his death, how he asked God's forgiveness for those who killed him, how he responded to the jeers of the crowd with compassion—well, something broke open in me. I believed it. I believed *him*. And I saw my life through his eyes. What a waste. Man, what a waste. But there I was, at the end of my life, and I wasn't dead yet, so what I had left, I gave. I really believed, and I really knew that if he was who he said he was, then I had a chance. I was pretty late figuring it out, but I made it just in the nick of time. That didn't make me gleeful for having led a sinful life that I got away with; it made me sorry I hadn't met him earlier. It made me wonder how my life might have been different if I had followed him sooner."

Maybe the reward isn't obtaining the promise of paradise; maybe the reward is having time with Jesus. If that is the case, then yes, the good thief most definitely missed out for almost the entirety of his earthly life, and that particular variety of missing out isn't one to envy. And if that was the case back then, it is likely still the case now. Our "heavenly reward" can be enjoyed long before we die if it consists of relationship with God. That relationship started the moment we were created and is shaped all throughout the course of our lives. Maybe this is why Jesus taught us to pray "your kingdom come, your will be done, on earth as in heaven" (Matt 6:10). He tells us in no uncertain terms that God's heavenly kingdom begins with our life here on earth. Being in relationship with God isn't a heavenly reward resulting from good behavior during our lifetimes. It is not something we earn or deserve; rather, relationship with God is something we must decide to recognize— and choose. God doesn't force us, but God never ceases having a home for us.

My friend Sara asked for help one summer Saturday cleaning out her garage and repainting it. She thought it was a small enough job that if we started early we could finish in time for her to treat me to a fancy dinner at an expensive restaurant nearby as a thank you. *That's* what I call a good motivator: steak and cheesecake. Halfway through the morning, we realized that "cleaning out" in and of itself would take most of the day, so she put in a call to her two nephews to come help with the painting, promising them a nice dinner out afterward as a thank you. OK, maybe the fancy restaurant wasn't still in the cards, but there would definitely still be steak. And cheesecake. By noontime, the next-door neighbor, having noticed that the project was progressing pretty slowly, offered to help cart away some of the junk, together with his daughter's Girl Scout troop. Fine; goodbye steak, but hello to a big juicy burger. And definitely still cheesecake. By the middle of the afternoon, with several of us working, the end was in sight, but it became clear that we wouldn't be able to cross the finish line by dinnertime. Sara called up her brother and his two roommates, who had run a 10K that morning, pleading for an hour's worth of help, and by 6:30 the job was done. The entire crew—now sixteen in number—collapsed on lawn chairs, grimy and exhausted but feeling quite fulfilled. We put in an order for pizzas to be delivered—*sans* cheesecake. The neighbor's wife and toddler joined us, Sara's sister and brother-in-law showed up to retrieve their sons, and the Girl Scout parents came to claim their daughters. Altogether, our little "garage band" had grown to about two dozen folks.

I would not call it virtue, the thing in me that failed to feel resentment for the lack of fancy steak and cheesecake. The only feeling that registered in me was sheer delight in the company of our little sweaty community unselfconsciously devouring the veggie lover's pizza and cheese sticks. Not one of us gathered in that circle had been "in it" for the beef, so to speak. We had been committed to the cause because of our relationship with Sara. While portioning out the pizza slices, no one thought, "It's not fair!" Nor did we calculate who deserved how much according to merit or exertion. Her nephews didn't resent the Girl Scouts for coming at noon, the neighbor didn't resent the runners for only showing up at the end, and Sara didn't mind the Girl Scout parents partaking of pizza just because it was available. It never was about the food on the table, the prize at the end—that served only as the center around which the fuller community gathered to celebrate. For me, and I venture to say for any one of us gathered around that circle, the entire endeavor was about our love for Sara and our commitment to the project she had undertaken. I knew all along that I was the lucky one, not because I had worked all day and "borne the day's heat," but because I was the first one she thought to call when she needed help. The fabric of our friendship, woven over years, was the true treasure (even more rewarding than cheesecake.)

When it comes to our relationship with God, why do we do the things we do? What's the purpose of being generous, kind, forgiving, loving? Is it to gain a prize, or is it done out of love for the God who *is* generosity, kindness, forgiveness, and love incarnate? If the motivation behind our acts of goodness is anything other than loving relationship with God and God's people, then we might be swimming in treacherous waters.

If my motivation in helping Sara had been the steak and cheesecake, then my day would have ended in indignation, resentment, and a sense of chagrin at all those who hadn't earned the thank-you dinner. Had this been my motivation and my response, my relationship with Sara certainly would have been altered, and not for the better. Furthermore, I would have had no interest whatsoever in developing a relationship with any of the "freeloaders" gathered around the yard. I would have been unable to perceive "those people" (always a dangerous phrase) as anything other than hindrances to the goal, undeserving and disgraceful moochers. Even if Sara had provided a fancy steak-and-cheesecake dinner for the entire crew, I doubt my indignation would have been appeased, as I would have looked askance at those who showed up at the end, measuring their contribution and judging their worthiness. If I had been "in it" for the reward, none of the relationships would have mattered. In fact, they would have suffered.

Isn't this the gift offered us as we witness the conversation at the place of the Skull? It's not about the worthiness of the good thief; it's not about the place he'll receive in paradise or whether or not he deserves it. It's about the God who welcomes him in and loves him into eternity, a full citizen of the heavenly kingdom. *That* is the God who loves each one of us and in whose "project" we are invited to participate.

We don't always get what we deserve—*thank God*. I remember talking with my sister Lucy about some of the burdens she was carrying at one point in her life. I perceived them at the time as being heavy, difficult, painful. She looked at me thoughtfully, appreciative, perhaps, of my sensitivity but somewhat saddened by my lack of understanding. She took the opportunity to teach me something that I still consider to be one of the keys to genuine happiness. She said, "I don't question the challenges God sends my way. If I did, I'd have to question the gifts, too."

Maybe the reason we so easily cry out "It's not fair" is because we identify with the aggrieved party. But what if we identified instead with the one who is granted the undeserved gift? What if, even beyond that, our focus was not on the undeserved gift but on the giver of gifts undeserved? Might that change our perspective on the entire situation? Might it even change our perspective on ourselves? We're all thieves of God's grace, being granted that which we haven't earned and don't fully deserve. But we receive it anyway—*because God is good.* Would you be willing to get your hands dirty working for that kind of God, even if it meant sharing your cheesecake with a latecomer?

Hard as it might be to accept, Jesus doesn't ask us to earn our heavenly reward; he asks us to be in relationship with him, to *follow him.* He invites us to weave a fabric of friendship with him, to be converted, to love, to forgive, to give without counting the cost. He introduces us to our God, who is lavish in mercy, indiscriminate in compassion, and eager to have a strong relationship with us. He promises us a kingdom, complete with converted thieves and returned prodigals, a place where, if we're completely honest with ourselves, we can feel right at home in their company. None of us deserves the kind of mercy and love God gives. Thank God we don't get what we deserve.

There were two thieves crucified with Jesus on Good Friday. One left this world spiteful and mean-spirited; the other left this world professing faith in the power of forgiveness and healing. And the God that hung between them offered what neither of them deserved. Only one question remains for those of us standing in witness to the scene, brooding over some version of "That's not fair!": Is our underlying emotion indignation? Or is it gratitude?

Afterword

I find it delightful that the first word of this book is *What?* and the last word is *gratitude*. That pretty much sums up the entire project of writing these pages. Life provides so many questions as we journey through our days, not the least of which concerns what this whole life "thing" is about anyway. There can be no single answer to the questions of purpose, ultimate meaning, or faith, but I have found that gratitude comes pretty darned close.

We have spent eight chapters meeting and engaging with a variety of gospel characters, each providing us with a story, a journey, and a gift. We have listened to them, accompanied them, and received their wisdom, and yet we still cannot call them by name. So be it. Maybe there is no lack in that reality; maybe that reality is itself another gift for which to give thanks. We are one family, brothers and sisters all, united in all our dazzling diversity. Who we are is important, but more important is *whose* we are. We belong to God—and we belong to one another.

Names are personal, but they are also limiting. I am Virginia. I am also daughter, friend, sister, teacher, student, aunt, disciple, sinner, and aspiring saint. Who are you? As you hold this book and approach its end, I know who you are. You are my brother, my sister. You are my companion and my friend, even if I won't know your name until we are together in eternity. You are God's and God is yours. And together, we are one.

Acknowledgments

From the first moment I considered this project, my mantra was "I don't know how to write a book," but thanks to many people, I have learned!

Thanks to Shannon, Peter, Stephanie, Jamie, and the entire team at Liturgical Press. You believed in me and took a chance on me. I am grateful.

Thanks to Ruth and Amy for being the very first cheerleaders encouraging me to write. You were my initial inspirations. I am grateful.

Thanks to Chris and Judi, Molly, Gene, and Sam. Together we formed the most vital, creative, collaborative, and integrity-laden team I have ever known. I am grateful.

Thanks to Mariette and Annie, Jen and Kate, Brooks and Cynthia, Annamarie, Missy, and Jenny for your input, insight, and friendship. You have each been faithful companions and beloved friends. I am grateful.

Thanks to Helen, Paul, Joan, Mark, Mary Ruth, Rose, John, Joe, Anne, Matt, Clare, and Lucy, my twelve older siblings. Because of you, our shared history, and your own families, I am who I am today and this book is what it is. I am grateful.

Thanks to my in-laws and all my nieces and nephews who are too numerous to name here. I was born into my family circumstances; you chose them. You are truly saintly, and I therefore lovingly add you to the ranks of characters in this book who are oh-so-very significant in my life. I am grateful.

Thanks to the community of the Sisters of St. Joseph of Carondelet (especially Joe, Sydney, and Sheila) for your kindness and hospitality as I wrote and rewrote, laughed and fretted, and ate lots of popcorn. I am grateful.

And special thanks to the Apostles of the Sacred Heart of Jesus, the religious community I have called home. You are and always will be my sisters in Christ, teaching me how to love from the Heart of Jesus. I am grateful.

Finally, thanks to Clelia and the love of her life, the Sacred Heart. The two of you are my most faithful and loving companions. I am beyond grateful.

Bibliography

Augustine of Hippo. *Confessions*, Book 8, Chapter 7. Translated by R.S. Pine-Coffin. London: Penguin, 1961.

Brueggemann, Walter. *The Message of the Psalms*. Minneapolis: Augsburg Fortress, 1984.

Catechism of the Catholic Church. 2nd ed. Washington, DC: United States Catholic Conference—Libreria Editrice Vaticana, 1997.

Eliot, George. *Middlemarch*. London: The Folio Society, 1999.

Herbers, Virginia. "Being Loved into Existence." *Global Sisters Report* (October 19, 2018). Available at https://www.global sistersreport.org/column/horizons/spirituality/being -loved-existence-55525.

Metzger, Bruce M. "Names for the Nameless." *The Oxford Companion to the Bible*. Edited by Bruce M. Metzger and Michael D. Coogan. *Oxford Biblical Studies Online*. Available at 10.1093 /acref/9780195046458.001.0001.

O'Day, Gail R. "Surprised by Faith: Jesus and the Canaanite Woman." *Listening/Journal of Religion and Culture* 24 (1989): 290–301.

P!nk. "What About Us." *Beautiful Trauma*. RCA, 2017, MP3.

ten Boom, Corrie. *The Hiding Place*. New York: Bantam, 1971.

Westermann, Claus. *Praise and Lament in the Psalms*. Atlanta: John Knox Press, 1981.